RE-ENTRY

RE-ENTRY

SURVIVING LIFE AFTER WAR

Michelle Matthews

iUniverse, Inc.
Bloomington

Re-entry
Surviving Life After War

iUniverse books may be ordered through booksellers or by contacting:

iUniverse
1663 Liberty Drive
Bloomington, IN 47403
www.iuniverse.com
1-800-Authors (1-800-288-4677)

ISBN: 978-1-4697-8468-7 (sc)
ISBN: 978-1-4697-8470-0 (hc)
ISBN: 978-1-4697-8469-4 (ebk)

Printed in the United States of America

iUniverse rev. date: 03/12/2012

CONTENTS

Michelle Matthews gives us a poignant account of the war in Iraq, its tragic aftermath and her courageous journey to heal emotionally. This is an important book to read for any veteran who is struggling with adapting back to civilian life and for those who want to understand the devastating impact that war has on our service men and women.

~Beth Chamblin, M.S.W., L.C.S.W.

To all the members of the United States military, active, reserve, and guard, retired and all veterans of war past and present. It is for them I write and give a voice to war and surviving it.

ACKNOWLEDGMENTS

My friend Beth for all her love and support. She invested time and she walked side by side with me on this journey. I could not have completed this without you.

Julie words cannot express my thanks.

My Mom and Dad for all their love. Thanks to all my family members. I came home broken and you helped put me back together.

My friends who loved and cared for me through my life before, during and after war. I am who I am because of each of you.

And to all at the Veterans Administration Hospital in St. Louis, Missouri. Dr. Siram Maitra, Dr. Julie Mastnak, Christina Fagan, MSW, and Nicole Bormann, MPT and Jean Ferguson CTRS. You cared for me when I couldn't. Thanks to all the hard working men and women at the VA for the dedication to past and present veterans of war. We are often not the best patients, and I value your dedication to serving us.

Introduction

The journey after war can be the toughest. During war I lived and breathed combat, leaving behind what I understood to be normal life. I acclimated to life in a war zone, learning to navigate through chaotic days and nights. War became my new identity. Because I normalized war, civilian life became the oddity.

Soldiers come home to find their minds still in combat. It is common to live on alert in a constant fight or flight state, addicted to adrenaline, overwhelmed by some of the simplest things (such as doing laundry or paying bills) and outraged at the complacency of the rest of world. Simple things became confusing and complex. *Why do people drive on the rights side of the road when I just want to drive down the middle of the road? Is that piece of trash on the side of the road a bomb?* We are trained to survive war. No one trains us to survive reentry.

Changes—in myself and others—became apparent as I spent more time at home. The life that once belonged to me was foreign. My loved ones were worried and scared for me but adjusted to life without me. I did not adjust to life without them. I wasn't ready for them to have gone on without me and I wasn't ready to talk about what had become my reality.

For several months I didn't understand war's impact on me. I thought I could step back into my former life and act as if I never went to Iraq. But the body remembers, and I found unhealthy ways to rid myself of the memories of war. I drank alcohol in excess, overate and over-exercised to relieve stress and anxiety. These were not healthy ways to cope with life after war but over time, and with a great deal of help, support and hard work, I began to find my way back to normal life.

We must open a dialogue about war and its cost to us and our relationships. We must give a voice to those who have lost theirs due to war. We must talk about things that we do not talk about, such as being afraid of our own thoughts of suicide or homicide. To write and talk about it is to risk it coming back to us, but it never really leaves anyhow.

Life after chaos is hard to navigate. War may make us, break us and change our lives, but we can make the choices to survive and live happily. Like many of life's journeys, it is possible to find hope in the struggle.

I do not want to address political ideologies or thoughts of being for or against war. Though I am ready to serve again, the reality of war is that it damages us as a nation, as a community and as individuals. Many veterans return with psychological problems, including depression and Post Traumatic Stress Disorder (PTSD). Experts say that 11-20 veterans out of 100 suffer from PTSD.[1] And those numbers represent only those men and women who report their symptoms and seek professional help. Many more do not report symptoms. If PTSD is not treated, some veterans turn to alcohol, drugs, suicide and other unhealthy ways of coping with their emotions. Professional help is a lifeline, but can only help after we make the decision to take control of our life and become a balanced person.

My experiences with war and its aftermath may be different from others. This is my story and journey. I am not "war," but it will always be a part of me. I encourage anyone who is suffering from war and its aftermath to find your voice, find yourself and take the journey to heal.

---

[1]   http://www.ptsd.va.gov/public/pages/how-common-is-ptsd.asp

BEFORE IRAQ

I joined the military the first time in 1986. I went on active duty and served for three and a half years overseas in Germany, learning a great deal about the Cold War and World War II. To have been in Germany when the Berlin Wall came down is indescribable. But soon I wanted a different direction in life, so I left active duty, joined the United States Army Reserve in Colorado, was honorably discharged and went to college to complete my degree in psychology.

After I graduated a friend informed me about a career opportunity in the Reserves. I reenlisted in 2001 and became a commissioned officer to work in public affairs. Just two months later our country was attacked by terrorists on September 11th. The world was forever changed and I was ready to deploy and defend our nation.

Because I was a Reservist, I also had a full-time position as a case manager at the health department in St. Louis. My military commitment was supposed to be only one weekend a month and two weeks in the summer, but it was never really like that. To become a commissioned officer, training is necessary that requires much more than just weekends. I struggled to fit it in with my other priorities: training for marathons and various races, an active family and social life, and of course looking for Mr. Right. I had my health; I was financially stable and I was truly happy. My life was a balance of ordinary and extraordinary—just the way I wanted it.

I was an enlisted soldier and was training at Fort Meade, Maryland in 2003 to be a videographer when my fellow soldiers and I watched the Iraq war unfold on television. We knew we were going to be part of the war effort. Some volunteered to go right away. Soldiers don't fight solely for a cause or for political ideologies: they fight for each other. As the weight of war was upon us, the camaraderie was amazing and uplifting.

But internally I thought, w*hat have we gotten ourselves into? Are we really at war?* The reality of war is death and destruction. The mission of serving and protecting our nation was weighted by a tremendous fear of death.

Perhaps I was in denial in the early stages: *the 1991 Iraq war was short—less than a month, right? There will be others to go first before it's over. I probably won't have to deploy.*

By the time I attended my Officer Basic Course in September of 2004 the U.S. was fighting in two wars. We were in Afghanistan and Iraq. Yet I still believed that they would be over soon and that I would not be needed. I could not envision myself going to war. I met returning soldiers who talked about their lives in Iraq and I could not relate to them because, I believed I wasn't going to share their experience. Rather it was because I had no real concept of war.

In October 2004 I learned by email from my mentor and commander that I was going to be deployed. At first I did not tell anyone that we were tasked to go because I still clung to the thought that it wouldn't be me.

I was selected to attend training in March 2005 for Improvised Explosive Device (IED) in Fort McCoy, Wisconsin. The training included identifying IEDs by type, by terrain, how they were made, what parts were used and how they were employed and used against the U.S. military. Countless videos documented what they looked like, how they sounded and their aftermath. An IED brings death and injury to anyone caught in its path. Learning about the destruction caused by IEDs brings war—and its casualties—to life. Reality was closing in.

I was training at Fort McCoy when I met a man and began a relationship. It was fate as far as I was concerned. He was going to war; I was going to war, so it was exactly what I needed at the time. I felt the overwhelming need to be in a relationship—to love, to be loved. I thought that being in love would change my outlook on war, somehow make it better.

Sexual harassment

Going to war was my major concern during this time, but there was another issue lurking in the background. An issue that would cause many more problems during deployment training and in Iraq. The commander who emailed my deployment orders had feelings for me in the past. He had previously served as my assigned mentor and had indicated his desire to have a romantic relationship. I made it clear that I found his advances unprofessional and did not want a relationship with him. Eventually he took a full time Active-Guard Reserve position in another state, so the situation seemed to take care of itself. When I received the email from him I assumed that through time, distances and life his interests, would no longer be focused on me.

As deployment neared, this commander called and emailed frequently to discuss deployment and ideas about training. He began flying into St. Louis and wanting to meet with me on the weekends. I felt uncomfortable, but ignored my reservations because he was maintaining professionalism. I found it odd that he always wanted to talk excessively to me about deployment and training. I was still dating the man I met in training at Fort McCoy and it became very clear that my commander was not happy with me having a relationship with another man. Once, while driving to a unit member's home to pick up equipment, he began asking me questions about my relationship and the seriousness of it.

"Why does it matter?" I asked.

"Because when we deploy you and I are going to be together all the time, like a married couple in love, so you might want to break up with him because he may not be able to handle our relationship."

I realized my discomfort was warranted. I made it clear once more that I didn't want a relationship with him, ever. Situations like this are painfully uncomfortable, and finding the easiest way out becomes the most viable solution. Mine was going to public affairs school—*I wouldn't have to deal with it there, right?* Never mind that he acted childish around me, singling me out in front of my peers. I would be living in Fort Meade, Maryland, nearer to my boyfriend. I focused on that.

While I was at Fort Meade my commander, who lived in New York, decided to come see me under the guise of introducing me to other unit members that were living in the New York area. He told me he was coming, but I told him that, due to my school commitments, I could not meet with them. He came to Fort Meade anyway, calling to say they were coming to pick me up for lunch. I felt uncomfortable being put in this position because he was my commander and I didn't want to appear uncooperative or anti-social to the new members of the unit.

While nothing happened at lunch that day, a few weeks later he came back unannounced. He called when he was almost to Fort Meade, leaving a voice mail that he was on post and coming to meet me. My friend Toni helped me get out of the area without running into him. Instead he talked to my instructors about my academic progress. He called several times and left numerous voice mail messages about meeting me for dinner. I couldn't answer my phone and avoided going home because friends and classmates warned me that a man claiming to be my commander was waiting in the hallway outside my door. Under normal circumstances addresses are not disclosed, but as my commander he could find me anywhere. I didn't go home until I received his voice mail that he was on his way back to New York.

My commander moved to St. Louis, my hometown. He continued calling and emailing constantly. He abused our relationship, beginning conversations talking about deployment, but quickly moving to talking about my relationship with my boyfriend. As my commander I was obligated to talk to him about work related issues, but didn't feel the need to disclose personal information about my boyfriend. Partly because of him, I decided to go to New Jersey and stay with my boyfriend after I graduated from public affairs school before returning to St. Louis.

Knowing I was in New Jersey, he requested that I go to his apartment in New York and pick up his mail to bring with me back to St. Louis. I objected, stating very clearly that I would not do that and he was abusing his authority. My boyfriend, also a military officer, was listening to the conversation and demanded to speak to my commander. He explained that my commander was being unprofessional and that he should leave me alone. That I was not interested in a relationship other than the one I was currently involved in. I don't know what was said on the other end, but my boyfriend told him to get his own mail and hung up the phone. The situation was infuriating, but since my boyfriend confronted him I thought he would back off.

I moved back home to St. Louis in July 2005 since my boyfriend was scheduled to deploy to Iraq in August. I was working at my unit and was relieved that my commander was acting professionally. I headed to El Paso, Texas to see my boyfriend who was deploying from there and he gave me a ring. The ring signified a future commitment of marriage.

When I returned to St. Louis with a ring on my finger my commander became angry and preached to me about how I should not get married before I deployed, because "my boyfriend would probably cheat on me or I would cheat on him." Then "I love you" slipped out of his mouth. I knew

I had to do something more than just telling him to leave me alone. I went to my chain of command. I was called into an office of a full Colonel and he told me he would talk to him and let me know the outcome. There was a meeting held and my commander seemed to understand the potential problems this was causing and agreed to leave me alone. That "leave me alone" period lasted about a month.

Everything started again once we left St. Louis to attend mobilization training at Fort Riley. He harassed me every chance he could. He said inappropriate things to me and about me to other members of the unit. For example, when we first arrived to Fort Riley and were looking around the barracks to determine room assignments he said in front of other unit members, "oh no worries I have a big room, she can stay with me." I told him his comment was inappropriate. Everyone else just laughed.

One afternoon we were at the Central Issue Facility (CIF) getting new boots, uniforms and equipment. I was wearing my newly issued boots when he walked up to me, grabbed my foot and began talking in baby talk saying "how cute my little wittle foot was in the boots." The people around me just laughed, but I was humiliated. It was the straw that broke the camel's back. I called the Colonel who I originally talked to about this in St. Louis and he instructed me to file a formal complaint against him. I was so angry that I immediately went to my higher command and began the process.

Email home September 18, 2005

> *I am not sure I can endure this anymore. His constant harassment is so out of control. I have tried to talk to him and I am trying to maintain my professionalism; it just doesn't seem to make a difference.*

The process to file a formal sexual harassment complaint is scary and difficult. Once the complaint is filed everyone in unit becomes subject to interviews and it is no longer a secret. Filing the complaint against my commander divided the unit. My commander was well liked and personal friends with most of the unit, and had hand-selected several of them to deploy with the unit. They were friends outside of work—there were few professional boundaries between him and some of the enlisted members of the unit.

Email home September 28, 2005

> *You may have already heard I filed a sexual harassment case against my commander and I am waiting for the investigation to start and the outcome. I am hoping to be home sooner than I think or maybe get sent to another unit. Say prayers. We will know what happens in about two weeks.*

Life got even more complicated after I filed the complaint. As a leader in a unit that was getting ready to deploy, I didn't need to be undermined or disrespected. But it had already happened and it continued to happen, despite my focus on maintaining professional behavior during final training to go to Iraq. There were several incidents when I would be conducting a briefing or training and snide remarks were made by unit members that were aligned with him. My commander was present when this occurred and allowed it to happen. I tried to correct the situation by asking my commander to restore discipline and order within in the unit. He ignored my requests. I was completely undermined as a leader. The unit was out of control, lacked discipline and we were not working as a team. I was alone in this fight, without the support in my unit or my higher command.

Email home September 29, 2005

> *It is all started now and things have gotten worse, couldn't believe that it could, but it has. Wish me luck, say prayers and know that I will try to remain strong. Harassed by him, harassed by unit members, doesn't feel like a good thing to be going on before I deploy to war. Love and miss you madly.*

During the investigation I was still assigned to the unit because the procedure requires the individual who makes the complaint remain in the unit (so it does not look like the person is being punished by being removed). In normal situations this process may be beneficial but since we were deploying to war and were at a mobilization training site, I had to work and live with unit members 24/7 without any relief. I was with people who truly didn't believe anything was wrong with his behavior. Some didn't believe me or thought I was "crazy." Some thought I was claiming sexual harassment to get out of deployment. Rumors, innuendos and gossip ran rampant. I was told not to discuss the case and followed these guidelines, but my commander and unit members discussed the case openly. I was an outcast.

My support came from my family and friends at home and an officer from another unit, Greg, who befriended me at the training site. I would call my family and friends every chance I could to talk about what was happening and to give them the latest updates on the investigation. By day twelve of the investigation I was at my breaking point. I was overwhelmed with anxiety and tired of being re-victimized over and over again by my unit members. I called my father to talk to him about what was happening and he became so angry that he wanted to call his congressman. I told him that I had two more days until the outcome and if it went past the time, he could make the call.

The investigation lasted fourteen days and it was the longest two weeks of my life. I went to my higher command to request a transfer to another unit while the investigation was going on because I could no longer be subjected to the constant harassment. It was very clear to me that whatever the outcome of the investigation, I was going to war with this unit. Not just to an annual training or a weekend drill, but to war which required unit cohesion and trust.

When the investigation was completed he was relieved of his command and recommended for an Article 15 (a form of reprimand pursuant to the Uniform Code of Military Justice). On the day he was relieved my unit was attending combat lifesaving training and I received a phone call informing me of the outcome of the investigation. When our training was over the unit marched back to the barracks to find the commander loading his bags into a van. Unit members rushed to him and began asking him questions. I could see that they were angry and physically upset because some of them were crying and I heard someone yell "this is bullshit."

After he drove away the unit went to the barracks common room. Some members were so angry they began to throw furniture around. I immediately went to headquarters and told them what was happening and a meeting was called that required the whole unit to attend. The commander from a higher headquarters briefed the unit on the outcome of the investigation and explained what happened, why it happened and what we as unit will and will not do. The Colonel laid out our new chain of command, told unit members if they had a problem with this decision that they needed to address her, and commanded us to "get back to training and stop the childish antics" before she walked out.

The next day I had to appear before the Colonel for her to read me the final results of the investigation and her punitive recommendations for his sexually harassing me. The investigation revealed that he called my cell phone approximately 250 times in a 45-day period and also called my mother's house more than 100 times. I learned that there were other witnesses outside of my unit that verified his harassment of me. I was so relieved that the system worked for me and that my complaints were validated.

Despite my relief, I begged the Colonel not to send me with the unit because of their loyalty to him. When he was relieved of his command people visibly wept. It was as though someone in our unit died. I was very serious about my request. I explained to her that I felt that there were bigger implications to this and those implications involved fratricide (soldiers killing their own), and though I didn't want to think that way about my unit members, I still had to consider it because we were going to war. She looked me directly in the eyes and told me, "You are going to be fine. No one will do that to you." She dismissed me so it was the end of the discussion. I walked out of her office defeated. Though I was validated in my complaint, I did not want to face those unit members and the possibilities of what could come from deployment. I was going to war with a unit that didn't like, respect or consider me a leader.

Fortunately I was able to hold on to my sanity during the investigation due to the support of my friend Greg. He heard rumors about what was happening and he reached out to me. We became good friends. He helped me through this distressing time and made me laugh by pointing out the absurdities of the situation. We continue a close friendship to this day and I can honestly say that if he wasn't around I do not think I would have emotionally survived this ordeal. His support continued through deployment and I am thankful for his friendship.

Life falters before deployment

There were other stressful circumstances happening in my life while I was dealing with the harassment from my commander. After my Improvised Explosive Device (IED) training and I realized what war looked like and it caused great anxiety. I was not ready for what I knew I would be facing.

Over a period of 4 days, I realized home life was falling apart into the chaos I had gotten used to in the military.

For reasons I still cannot explain, my roommate (and friend) kicked me out of the house we shared. Our friendship ended in her screaming tirade, with me locked in my room afraid to confront her. I knew she struggled with emotional problems so I tried to be patient. Her family members were friends (so I thought) and I hoped they would intervene. Instead, they locked me out of the house, unable to get my things. It was embarrassing and frustrating to be treated like a criminal. When they agreed to let me back in and move out, friends and family helped me gather my things quickly and move them out.

When you go to war, you know the reality is you might not come back. You don't want to burden your family with more than is necessary. You try to plan carefully what to leave behind. But with my things being taken so quickly from my house, I just gave them away. Sadly, I still don't know what was left behind or what should have been saved.

The day after I was locked out of my house, I received my orders by fax. I just stared at them. My name and social security number were there; it was actually *me* that was going. It finally sunk in that I was heading to a war zone. There aren't words to describe that feeling. You train, prepare, plan . . . and you're never really ready. I thought *this could be it for me. What have I done with my life? How will I say goodbye? What will happen to me, my unit, my family and friends?*

There were so many questions without answers. Tears fell on the orders. My understanding of war was based on movies, books, and actual footage as well as war veterans. I knew war involved sadness, pain, injury and possibly death. Of course nothing prepares you for what you actually live.

When the orders actually arrived, I began to think about my life differently. I was happily single and suddenly wanted to be married. I also wanted children. The "what ifs" of life filled my mind: *what if I die before I get married, have children and travel to those places on my "bucket list?" Who will take care of me if I get injured physically or psychologically?* I couldn't answer any of them and this made me feel desperately out of control.

I called my family and friends to let them know that I was going to war. Their reactions ranged from silence to dismissive to tears. I told them directly, without any emotion or feelings. At work I talked to my co-workers and acted normal. Outwardly I appeared calm and cool, but inwardly I was anxious and overwhelmed. I was scared and sad for myself and my family and friends. Expressing fear could make me seem weak. So I was outwardly strong but internally falling apart.

The day after I received my definitive orders for war I was laid off. My boss handed a few of us our pink slips and told us that our last day at work would be April 21ˢᵗ. Somehow, in three days, I was homeless, jobless and going to war. I wondered if life could get any worse. Several months later, before returning, I sent an email to the City of St. Louis to ask what recourse I had for gaining my job back. They said I had none, and asked me not to contact them again. It seemed unnecessarily mean.

Luckily, I found a place to stay at a friend's house and had only a couple weeks before having to report for training, so I wasn't out of work long. But it was hard to focus on the positive. I was depressed and confused. Every day I woke up questioning why all of these bad things were happening to me at the same time. I wanted to run away, lie down and just fall apart. Life before leaving was supposed to be routine. Instead all these rapid changes made my anxiety much worse.

I visited with friends in Colorado to escape my current situation. My friend's husband was a retired Marine and served in Vietnam, so I talked to him about war and my concerns. It felt good to just let it out with someone who understood. I also took time to get my life in order. I organized my storage unit and labeled my boxes so that, if I died or was physically injured, my family could easily locate necessary or sentimental items without added stress. That was a difficult task. I sat among my belongings and wondered, *is this how I will be remembered?*

Training

The first training I was selected to attend was the aforementioned IED training at Fort McCoy, Wisconsin in March 2005. This training opened my eyes to the reality of what the war in Iraq looked like. Though I heard about IEDs on the news and saw various video clips, it was this training that helped me understand what an IED looked like and its aftermath. I talked to soldiers who were injured by them or had their soldiers killed by them. We learned how they were made, how to identify them and what to do if you or your vehicle is hit by one. During the training, I asked questions about Iraq and IEDs. My focus became IEDs. I read everything I could and soaked up all the information available. Once I finished the training, I had to go back to my unit and train them on this important subject.

That training answered many of my questions about war: war was ugly and it was hell. People lived on constant alert, were injured, and died. There were IED attacks on convoys, Vehicle Born Improvised Explosive Devices (VBIED) and sniper fire. It was overwhelming to watch and hear about war. I never worried about any of these things living in the United States, but I was going to the country of IEDs, insecurity and chaos, which was a far cry from my experiences as an American. This training heightened my sense of awareness regarding war and Iraq.

I met soldiers who returned from Iraq who shared stories about barely escaping death and others who were killed or injured by roadside bombs. It was a country that lived under a dictatorship for so long and was backwards by our standards. It was a place where clean water, proper waste management and basic ideas of liberty and equality did not exist. This training reinforced my beliefs about war and death.

When I returned to my unit, I was an expert on IEDs. I took this training seriously and incorporated it into all trainings. I talked constantly about situational awareness and looking at your surroundings. During training at Fort Riley I set up a practical exercise to identify IEDs. I focused on scanning your area to identify potential IEDs, looking for items out of place like tires in the middle of the road or wires sticking out of trash piles. The rule was to scan the perimeter 5 feet to 25 feet as you walked or drove a vehicle. My mantra became "5 and 25 stay alert and stay alive." Being aware of your surroundings and knowing what to look for was the way to keep yourself and others safe.

Public Affairs Training

My public affairs training in Fort Meade, Maryland prepared me for my future position in Iraq. The school was academically rigorous and intense because a four year journalism degree was squeezed into a nine-week course. I didn't have a job or home, so packing my car was not a problem, but I would be away from family and friends and that bothered me. I wanted to spend as much time with them before I deployed. Soldiers almost always have lengthy training prior to deployment, and it just makes our displacement that much longer.

During school I met some amazing officers from the Army, Air Force, Navy, Coast Guard and civilians. I learned a great deal from them about public affairs. It was funny to me that when I told someone I was deploying to a war zone I got responses like, "good for you, good for your career, it is a piece of cake." I asked if they or anyone they knew had been or could still be in Baghdad, but they didn't.

I was in journalism school so I focused on the media. I began to watch the news frequently and learned about the death and destruction in Iraq. My imagination of war played out on television, adding to my anxiety. *I do not want it to be me. I do not want it to be anyone.* I felt isolated because most of the people around me weren't deploying so I had no one to discuss my feelings with. There were many days when I was unable to sleep or concentrate.

My saving grace in Fort Meade was being closer to my boyfriend who lived in New Jersey. Our relationship intensified while I was there and I fell in love with him. Our deployment to Iraq was our common bond. He was entering the same unknown world as I was. In hindsight, maybe I was in love with him or maybe I was just afraid that I would die alone, without love. It made perfect sense at the time to be involved with someone who was going to the same place I was and could support me while I was there.

Getting closer to war

By mid-August my unit began training full-time and worked long days and nights. My life was consumed with the military and training for Iraq. We had a legal briefing about creating our wills/living wills and power of attorney. The person giving the briefing said to us "Remember to get all your affairs in order before you leave so you do not burden your family. If you do not return, it will make it easier for them to deal with your personal belongings." I remember feeling sick to my stomach and tears welled up in my eyes. I left the room and went directly to the bathroom. I felt my heart break and I had difficulty thinking. I had to show leadership; I had to get it together. I pulled myself up and gathered the soldiers in my unit and gave them 24 hours to figure out what they were going to do with their belongings. We needed to make sure that our families were not burdened.

My belongings were well organized in the storage unit. Boxes were filled with knickknacks and pictures that had names on them. These items were things each of them gave me over the years that should be returned to them if I didn't come home. I hoped by having saved them they would know I loved them. I saved things like my niece's pictures she drew in kindergarten. There was a box that contained a lovely vase that my friend Dinorah gave me that I wanted to be sure she got back. The content of the boxes was my way of telling each of them that I loved them and to never forget me.

Since I was working such long hours it was very difficult to spend much time with friends or family. We were training and being evaluated before we left for our mobilization site in Fort Riley, Kansas. My sense of urgency with them was not always reciprocated or understood. I think many of my friends and family members were in denial about me going to war and often dismissed my feelings. Maybe they just didn't know how to respond. One day I was off of work early and eager to spend time with friends. I wanted to see them and tell them that I loved them and be sure they knew how much they meant to me. I couldn't reach any of them, so I left messages. I told them I love them and miss them and if I didn't see them again, I appreciate their friendship.

A friend of mine called me back and told me I was crazy for leaving her such a message.

"Of course you are coming back, don't be so overly dramatic!" she said.

"But what if I don't?"

She responded with silence, then a little laugh and then anger. "You are coming back, so don't leave me a message like that again!" I was stunned and couldn't understand why she was so upset. I'm an optimist by nature, but there was a real possibility that I wouldn't return and it was important for my friends to know how much I truly valued them. I needed my potential last words to be "I love you, we had great times together and I treasure our friendship." While I wasn't planning my death, I was trying to prepare myself and loved ones for that possibility.

Mobilization training

We completed our home station training by the middle of September and departed to our mobilization site at Fort Riley, Kansas. The training intensified and we were evaluated as a unit to determine whether we could successfully deploy to a theater of war. The training covered weapons training, IED awareness, Humvee roll-over training and battle field life saving techniques. I attended additional briefings regarding legal issues, living wills and power of attorneys. We each had to get numerous shots and vaccinations including hepatitis A, B and small pox. We trained seven days a week and there was minimal down time. I lived with a roommate and slept on a bunk bed. I had to walk down a long hallway to shower and I had to walk about 4 blocks to get meals in the cold, rain and snow. The conveniences of home life were taken away and the life that I knew was gone.

Our training was very intense. As a unit we were introduced to new tactics and techniques in about every area of combat operations. The training became more critical and we were evaluated at every step. Our evaluators always commented on our unit's lack of teamwork but could not express their observations until after the commander who sexually harassed me was relieved. The evaluators assessed that the unit's lack of cohesion was due to the commander's inability to lead effectively.

We were issued new uniforms, new boots, helmets and a plated vest that weighed 22 pounds or more. We needed to learn how to walk and work with the vest on and it was physically challenging. Each day we trained more and more. Equipment and responsibilities were added to our list of things to do. I tried to remain focused and involved in the training, but it was so overwhelming. I sought solace in talking to the chaplain, but it didn't work. I often left the barracks to walk and walk until I was exhausted and fell asleep. I was going to sick call for headaches, gastrointestinal problems, and foot problems. I woke in the morning feeling like I had been hit by a truck and would head to the medical facility. Stress was taking its toll on me. I continued to train and learn as much as I could, but life had become so imbalanced.

In November we had our final evaluation exercise. This involved a series of events that had to be completed to get certified as a unit to go to war. One of our final evaluated trainings was to conduct a live fire from a moving vehicle. We had never encountered this before but it was significant because this was how we would fight in Iraq. This was how to fight in an urban fighting environment. On a 5-degree day we rode in Humvees that had no heat in them or in open air trucks. The wind was strong. I ended up in the hospital with frostbitten toes, hypothermia and a core temperature of 96 degrees.

My spirit was slowly dying. My belief in the Army and its values was nearly gone and now I was physically broken. Frostbite and hypothermia are things that remain problems for me and will for the rest of my life. I was released from the hospital and was sent back to the barracks to recover. All I could do was cry. I felt like I was living in Hell and I hadn't even seen Iraq yet.

The unit received a four day pass for the Thanksgiving weekend. I rented a vehicle for the five or so hours' drive home. It was my last trip home before departing for Iraq, so I was excited to see everyone one last time. Since I didn't really have a home of my own anymore, I stayed at a hotel. I could have stayed with friends or family but I was burned out on living with other people. I wanted time alone. The conditions I had been living in were less than ideal. The barracks were built during World War II. Black soot poured of out the heating vents, the heat never went off and you could not open a window. I lived with a roommate whom I secretly called "pigpen." Her half of the room was filled with trash, empty water bottles, snack wrappers and dirty laundry. I really needed a real bed, a real shower, cleanliness and space.

I also needed to sort through the last years of my life. If I died while at war, I wanted to be at peace. The harassment that I suffered from my commander and some of my unit members left me feeling emotionally fragile and vulnerable. I was still experiencing harassment from some of the former commander's loyal friends.

In this time alone I realized some things. I didn't have a job or a home and I was heading to a war zone, so I had less responsibility. I felt like I no longer had to worry about a "normal life" because if I died, none of this would matter. I felt a small sense of peace and relief. Maybe this is what it feels like when someone decides to commit suicide—they feel a sense of relief after making their decision. Though I wasn't suicidal, I needed to let go of my normal life.

During the three-and-a-half days I was home I was very busy. There were several "going away" events planned for me—parties, lunches, dinners. It was sort of ironic. The people I had wanted to spend time with so badly before, who couldn't find the time, now had my dance card full for my last 72 hours home. By then all I really wanted to do was sleep. I was eating, drinking and enjoying everyone's company. It looked like a celebration, but it really wasn't for me.

The first glimpse of the effects of war were seen at one "going away" lunch with friends and family on the Saturday before I had to go back to Fort Riley. I describe that lunch as the "last supper." I was stressed, tired and very scared. I wavered between being happy to see everyone and a sense of dread because it could be the last time. My mother seemed to be in an emotional coma and she just smiled and spoke on occasion. Everyone was dressed up, eating in a beautiful restaurant and celebrating me going off to war. Gifts and cards were exchanged; toasts were made in my honor. It was confusing because it felt like an average birthday or graduation celebration instead of a "good-bye and good luck in Iraq" event. It seemed a strange thing to celebrate. No one really knew what to do and other family and friends of service members were probably in the same predicament.

I met some friends for coffee to say one last farewell. We said our goodbyes and I drove away in the rental Dodge pickup truck that was the biggest truck I had ever driven. Somewhere past Kansas City the weather turned from cold to freezing and there was snow and black ice on the roads. I was driving about 25 miles per hour and I looked ahead of me and watched an 18-wheeler truck slide off into the median. A big patch of black ice was in front of me. I tried to slow down but I hit it as well and I did a 180-degree turn and ended up facing oncoming traffic. Another 18-wheeler passed me and missed the truck by a fourth of an inch. I sat paralyzed for about five seconds and then tried to figure out what to do.

I drove the opposite way on the shoulder and drove up the on-ramp the wrong way. I turned around and got back on the highway and called my dad. I was in a shear panic. My father calmed me down, but he didn't understand why I was so upset. I almost died and he just told me to calm down and stop being so dramatic. His response shocked me. I was looking for compassion, understanding and love. I was screaming inside, *Someone please help me. Save me from myself. Save me from war!* But I got my father telling me to calm down. My reaction to this event was not normal, but I was not "normal" anymore. Under normal circumstances, my father's words would have calmed me down. Instead I was overwhelmed and scared. I was not ready for my life.

We had a new commander upon returning to Fort Riley. He had a week to get to know us, figure out how to get us to work as a team and take us to war. He had his work cut out for him.

Family, friends and war

Our unit's Family Readiness Group (FRG) formed. This group is designed for family members to get to know one another, support each other and stay in touch with the unit. If they had questions or needed help, the group would support them. Our families were involved in the process of war as well. Since I was a Reservist, my family and friends were not as actively engaged in the military as active duty family members would be, so being thrust into the process of war was overwhelming for them. They had a vague idea of what I did, but these activities were baptism by fire. Military language is a barrier, as is leaving your loved one behind to go to war.

The Family Readiness Group held a meeting to talk about the role of the group, the support group itself and to convey information about what we might experience when we went to war. Many of my friends and family members attended the meeting. At one point they were shown a video. I am not sure where the video came from or the name of it, but the video showed soldiers getting manicures and their hair cut in a beauty salon and working out in fitness centers. It made Iraq appear to be relaxing and fun. I guess the military wanted to make family members and friends of military members feel better about the conditions of war. I understand the need to put loved ones at ease, but the information conveyed to them was sugar-coated and did not portray most soldiers' experiences with war.

The meeting succeeded in placating many family members and friends. My brother believed the video and my higher command. He did not understand what war was and the meeting did not explain its realities. My friend Beth said she felt very confused about the meeting. What she knew about Iraq from her own research and the video conflicted.

My parents, however, understood war from a different perspective. My paternal grandfather died in WWII, so my dad understood the reality that people die in wars. He watched the news and educated himself about Iraq—its politics, the people and their religion. He learned as much as he could to discuss my future assignment with me. I was heading to a war zone, away from their care. They had no control or say in the matter. They trusted me, they trusted the military, but they did not trust war. He held up strong, but I had never seen my father cry until I left for war. My mother was emotionally exhausted and sunk into a depression. She tried to remain strong for me and did a great job, but inside she was dying. I could see the pain on my parents' faces. It was as if the war had consumed their lives. They, like me, internalized it. They tried to show me their strength and I did the same for them. It was a mask we wore for each other to survive.

When I came home from Iraq, Beth asked me about this video. I told her that beauty shops, coffee shops, fitness centers and a base exchange existed but that not everyone got to enjoy those amenities. Even those who did were surrounded by mortars landing, gunshots, helicopters flying overhead, loud booms, black smoke; sand storms and 124 degree weather outside. That was the reality of war in Iraq. It seems some key elements were left out of the video.

Heading to war

We left for Kuwait on December 2nd, 2005. It was cold and snowing heavily. I wanted the flight to be delayed but it wasn't. The flight was a civilian plane with regular pilots and attendants, but it was filled with soldiers. I made a few last phone calls before I turned my cell phone off for good. My last phone call was to my mom and dad while I was standing in the front of the plane. I told them I loved them. I could hear their hearts break over the phone. My heart broke with theirs, but I am a soldier and a leader so I turned off those emotions. I was heading to war and it was time to stuff my fears and sorrow deep inside and focus on my mission. So I did. I dried my tears and sat down. I was ready to face the unknown.

On the plane I sat in the front next to a First Sergeant who I questioned about Iraq because it was his second time going. He did not want to talk to me about anything. He turned his back on me and went to sleep. I finally fell asleep and slept for about 8 hours. It was the first time I had slept that long in months. I woke up about an hour before we landed in Kuwait. Others on the plane were sleeping and reading and it might have seemed normal if I wasn't holding my M-16 across my lap and the man next to me sitting with his M-4 on his lap and 9 millimeter strapped to his thigh. We landed in Kuwait. Phase two of war began.

Kuwait: Welcome to War

Just when I thought my living conditions could not get any worse than the ancient barracks at Fort Riley, I arrived in Kuwait. Suddenly I understood that the comforts I was accustomed to were gone. Fort Riley was, by comparison, a five-star hotel.

We were taken off the plane and piled into large buses with drawn curtains. They could not be opened because we were United States soldiers entering the Middle East and due to the political situation our lives could be at risk. I immediately lost my sense of security and safety. I had my weapon with me, but none of us had ammunition. The buses moved slowly through main roads and then there were no roads, just tracks in the sand. I was so wired that I could hardly sit still, yet I was so exhausted that I could hardly keep my head up. I took many peeks outside because the curtains moved with the bus. I viewed oil fields and miles and miles of dirty sand. There was a horrible stench of burning gas/oil in the air. I didn't see a tree or color in any of the landscape. I was very unsettled by the fact that we had to be hidden. I had never been afraid of being an American soldier and I was insulted. I am an American, from the land of the free and the home of the brave—not someone to be hated.

We made a stop to use the bathroom and stretch our legs. The sand looked like a big litter box and smelled even worse. Porta-potties lined a small area and I thought, *why would anyone want to live here?* I immediately became aware of my judgmental attitude. Since I was raised in the United States it made me feel slightly superior. It was going to be hard for me to adjust to war in the Middle East. I was in Kuwait for less than two hours and already wrestling with my American pride and judgment of a country I knew nothing about.

The bus drivers were Middle Eastern and drank chai tea and smoked cigarettes while talking to each other. One of them offered me tea. He spoke half in English and half in Arabic. I had no idea what he was asking or why he asked me. In Arabic culture it in not customary for men to ask women to have tea, so I had no idea how to respond. I smiled and walked away, and asked another soldier why I was asked to have tea. He explained that this was the way their culture forms relationships. I would learn how valuable this small gesture was when I arrived in Iraq.

We arrived at Camp Buehring as the sun set. We exited the bus and I saw miles of sand, large white tents and more porta-potties. The smell in the air had changed. It was a combination of human waste, burning oil, gas and hot air. The smell was so pungent that it made me want to vomit. Overtime, I got used to it, but I will never forget it.

We were escorted inside a large tent and waited for further instructions. We learned that we were not on anyone's manifest rosters to arrive. There was a great deal of confusion and disorganization. This worried me because if no one knew were coming, how would we be supported? Eventually we attended a briefing, filled out lots of paperwork and got our military identification cards swiped. This told the "system" we had arrived in Kuwait.

We unloaded the buses for the "duffle bag drag" to our assigned tent. Since no one knew were coming we didn't have a place to sleep, so we were assigned one tent for the whole unit (men and women). Men and women were always separated in my experience. It seems in war many rules are thrown out or not enforced in order to do what is necessary. I was so exhausted and jet-lagged it didn't matter who was sleeping where, I just wanted to sleep. I could hardly focus and I fell asleep quickly.

I awakened quickly by the bright sun shining through the white tent. Even with air conditioning, it was nearly 100 degrees inside the tent. This was our welcome to Kuwait. We lived with the men for three days. It really was not much different than living in a tent with women only; people still snored, farted and talked in their sleep. We all were jet-lagged and found it difficult to get into a good sleep pattern. It took me about a week to adjust.

We were left to fend for ourselves so we decided as a unit to explore the area and locate key survival facilities. We located dining facilities, medical facilities and showers. Porta-potties were everywhere. We were not sure how long we would remain in Kuwait so we needed to orient ourselves to the area and make contact with people who could assist us with mitigating pre-war requirements. I heard a rumor that there were actual toilets that flushed with running water. I was on a quest to find those bathrooms. I located them about a mile away from our tent site, only to find they were off-limits to us "transient" people.

I didn't care that the bathrooms were for people stationed there. I thought if I could just feel normal for five minutes it would be worth the risk of punishment. There were real showers and real toilets and even washers and dryers. Those small things reminded you of home and normalcy, but because they were restricted I found it mildly absurd.

Meeting our Active Duty Counterpart

On the fifth day we met the Active Duty section we would be working with. We went to the meeting wearing our Desert Combat Uniforms (DCUs) while they were in their Army Combat Uniforms (ACUs). Looks of disappointment and disgust greeted us when we walked into the tent. We were not dressed like them. Additionally, we were Reservists and therefore not seen as "real" soldiers. It felt like showing up at a black-tie event in overalls and cowboy boots. There is an assumption by active component that reserve component would be untrained, undisciplined and unprofessional. When we arrived without notice on any manifest or roster and tried for days to make contact with our section, no one from the active side attempted to assist us. These factors started us out shaky and it didn't get better.

I know war isn't rainbows and sunshine, but I believe that when you meet people that you are going to work, eat, sleep and possibly die with there might be time for some kindness, communication and compassion. *Does war change us, or just make us who we really are?* I wrestled with that question the rest of my deployment.

We were in Kuwait for three weeks. Our active duty component limited the information they shared with us and made it very difficult to work or "bond" before we deployed into a war zone. It always seemed that we would be late for something or not prepared for the required training. We had daily meetings and things started to come together, but when we met the head of our section and he told us that he didn't expect much from us because we were the United States Army Reserve National Guard. I was dumbfounded by his lack of understanding of the Reserves and our role in the big picture. The United States Army Reserves is part of the Army. Somehow he combined the Reserves and National Guard. The National

Guard supports its state (it does get called to support the active Army) and the Reserves supports the active Army. Once again the disorganization, the lack of communication, and the hostile attitude towards our unit, made for a bad combination. We were not even at war yet and the internal war began.

Living conditions

The conditions in Kuwait were a shock to our systems. The sand, heat and the smells were overwhelming. Sand storms happened fairly regularly. You can never escape the sand. It is so microscopic that it goes in and on every part of your body. Americans are not used to living in desert conditions and aren't familiar with sand-borne illnesses. We were introduced to respiratory issues and skin problems created by the sand and to sand fleas, rodents and bugs we never knew existed. In the first two weeks, we had four people get sick from what is called the "Kuwaiti crud," a sand-borne illness that is a form of bronchitis caused by exposure to microbes in the sand and dust. Symptoms include 102 degree fevers and coughing up green mucus. At home when you are sick, you have a bed and maybe someone to take care of you. In Kuwait, you sleep on a cot with many other sick people around you and it is hot, dirty and dusty. Many other of my unit members got eye infections and we were all exhausted from the heat. I was one of the lucky ones who did not get sick in Kuwait.

There were about forty thousand people crammed into this area. There were groups arriving and departing every day. Anywhere you went there was a line or people walking or standing around. There was a Base Exchange (BX) that had various food, clothing and toiletry items. I stood outside in the heat and waited in line for two hours only to find the shelves almost bare and the shower shoes sold out. I wanted shower shoes so badly it was worth standing outside in 100 degree plus weather. I had already managed to lose two pair in less than a week. It was hard to focus in this new world and I always forgot something important like a towel or soap or would leave something like my shower shoes or uniform in the shower trailer.

I started marking my days based on the number of times I got to use the real bathroom and whether or not I took a shower. Those days were good days. Some days, there was no water in the shower trailer and you went without. I learned how valuable baby wipes are. They are a valuable commodity to those going to war.

When I experienced my first sandstorm I found myself buried to my waist in sand. I pulled myself out and tried to shake the sand off my body but it stuck to me. All I wanted to do was to take a shower and remove the sand from my body. I stood in the shower scraping the sand off me when I heard a loud gurgling sound coming from the pipes. Suddenly dirty and rancid-smelling water backed up into the shower trailer. The water gushed out of the drains and before I could react, I began vomiting. I threw up until the water went back down and I finished my shower. I had to—I was covered in soap, sand, dirty shower water and puke. When I walked outside the sand clung to me immediately and I felt just as dirty as I did before I took the shower.

I woke up one morning at 4:30 needing to use the bathroom. With my flashlight I spied some kind of rodent running towards the group of porta—potties I was heading too. I let out a little shriek. I heard some laughter and looked to find a man sitting on a bench smoking a cigarette. He said the rodent was a "shit-eating rat" and that they were everywhere and probably having dinner inside the toilet I was heading to. I was horrified. I had to go to the bathroom badly but I turned and walk another half mile to other porta-potties. I could not imagine a rat jumping out of the toilet on me. So I learned the lesson early: always rattle the doors or kick the sides to make sure the rats run out before you go in.

I worried about the dirty conditions of the porta-potties. There was pornographic graffiti all over the walls; men masturbated inside and left their semen marks. Once after using the bathroom I felt something slippery on the door lock. I soon figured out what it was. I wanted to scream, but I could only get my toilet paper and hand sanitizer out and go about my day. All our common humanness was exposed. I was used to running water, having privacy, sleeping in a nice bed, and eating good food with a nice glass of wine. Now I was sleeping in a tent on a cot with 125-degree temperatures and horrible bathroom conditions. I was walking for miles to find a toilet that wasn't overflowing with feces and urine. I was in a shithole.

There were trainings we had to complete while we were in Kuwait. We qualified with our weapons one last time before we deployed to Iraq.

Three weeks came and went and we were finally heading to war. If Kuwait was any indication of what Iraq was going to be like, then it was going to be a long, hard year. My anxiety was peppered with uncertainty and fear. Kuwait prepared me for the living conditions in Iraq, but all the training in the world can never really train you for war.

IRAQ

The flight from Kuwait to Iraq felt like the longest of my life. I wanted to get there and get it over with. I had already lost nearly a year of my life just training for this. We crammed into a military plane with all of our combat gear, making for an uncomfortable flight. The pilot informed us we would land in ten minutes and needed to have all our gear on to prepare for a combat landing. I looked to my fellow soldiers. Some looked scared, others had no expression. The plane dipped and swerved. I thought I might throw up. Combat landings are not for the weak at heart. I made eye contact with another soldier sitting on the side of the plane and all I could do was shake my head because he looked like I felt. No words were necessary to describe this fear. The fear was war.

I exited the plane and looked around. There was a large airport runway to the right of us. There were large tents and lots of sand. I was told we were across from the Baghdad International Airport. This area is where I would be working and living. It was 26-mile military base with various units stationed all around it. There were Blackhawk helicopters flying overhead and parked on the runway. It looked like a scene out of a movie. As we waited I saw the Blackhawks moving. I am not sure what I was thinking but I grabbed my camera and snapped a photo. I heard someone yell, "You are not allowed to take pictures of the helicopters!" I remembered: this is not vacation. This is war.

Training at Fort Riley and Kuwait prepared us for our living conditions in Iraq, but nothing could have trained me for war. Approximately 200 soldiers lined up on the runway waiting for instructions. Swiping my military identification card into the system identified me as being in a war zone and determined my pay. I learned that once we arrive in a theater of war we receive additional sums of money that included hazardous duty pay and hostile fire pay. I couldn't wrap my mind around this concept. I stood waiting for my identification card to be returned, watching people laughing and joking. I was confused about how to think or act. We were moved to our temporary living area which consisted of numerous tents set up in the middle of the field with shower trailers and bathrooms. The area was called "tent city."

Like Kuwait, Iraq is sand and dirt. But there were new hazards to worry about beyond sand fleas or shit-eating rats. They included mortars, rockets, gun fire and numerous other dangers. It wouldn't take long for me to experience these hazards.

First month in Iraq

We moved into tent city. I had to figure out how to take a shower, eat meals and find my way around the area. I moved into to a tent with 50 women. It was crowded and loud. Lights stayed on for 24 hours a day and people were coming in or out of the tent all the time. Tension was always high and verbal fights broke out regularly. There was the group of women who were leaving and were all very happy. They oozed happiness because, as one woman said, "I am leaving this hell hole."

I didn't fight or have issues with anyone, but I witnessed it. Sometimes I sat on my cot, looked around and said to myself, *am I really here, or is this a bad dream?* It was all surreal. I was used to training exercises and sleeping on a cot, but this was different because war was now my home. I missed my privacy. I was already used to having to walk outside to take a shower and go to the bathroom. I understood that I may get only cold water or no water at all for a shower. I never mastered my timing with showers in Kuwait and it wasn't going to change now that I was in Iraq.

On my second day in Iraq, I was standing in the shower area when several mortars landed and exploded close by. Everyone looked scared but no one reacted. I saw tears in the eyes of a young soldier. I walked over to her and smiled and told her it was going to be okay. I had no idea if it was going to be, but the least I could do was comfort her and I until the next one landed.

Mortars landed all around us. We saw large plumes of black smoke and heard gun shots, loud booms, and strange noises that continued 24 hours a day. I was introduced to the Muslim call to prayer and Arabic music floating through the air waves. All this was a constant reminder that I was no longer in United States.

Routine with a twist

I got used to carrying my weapon to the shower and bathroom with me. I had the most difficult time with my weapon in the bathroom. I would try to sling it over my shoulder and sit down to go to the bathroom, only to have it slip down and smack me in the back or hit me in the head. It was a routine I finally adjusted to, but it came with lots of bumps and bruises. Our weapons never left our sides.

On the third day in Iraq, I learned that there were shuttles that could take us across the base. I waited at a shuttle stop, assuming the shuttle would take me somewhere close to my work site. I also thought that there would be other soldiers on the shuttle I could ask about directions. Instead I was the only American soldier on the shuttle. No one spoke English. I was on a shuttle to somewhere and I had no idea where I was. I didn't have a cell phone or a way to communicate. The shuttle just drove from one point to another. People got on and off. I just stayed on looking for anything that was familiar. I stayed on that shuttle for about 30 minutes until I finally recognized an area. I yelled "stop" and jumped out of the shuttle. I made it to my work area but was very late. I learned that those shuttles were for the third country nationals who worked there and that there were other shuttles for soldiers. To say the least, it was uncomfortable. I had a weapon and no one was hostile to me, but I was unused to my surroundings and felt lost. Eventually I found the correct shuttles and took them to the areas I needed to be.

Mortars landed near tent city on a daily basis, usually at the same time during the day and night. These attacks happened every day. I didn't know where it was coming from, but I knew and understood that it was the enemy firing at us with the hopes of killing as many of us as they could. That was my instinct. As I started to get familiar with "war language," I learned that when a new unit arrives and were unfamiliar with enemy tactics the enemy saw this as an opportunity to take advantage of the new arrivals. We lost quite a few soldiers during the first few weeks of being in Iraq.

After three weeks we moved into single wide trailers divided into three living spaces. We call them our "hooch." There was nothing fancy about these accommodations—wood floors, panel walls, and a bed and wall locker. I initially moved in with a roommate so there was very little space.

I had two inches to walk between my bed and wall locker. Our belongings were piled on the floor, wall locker or on top of the bed.

Living in this trailer was unpleasant. To my surprise the tent was a much better living environment. We were cramped and on different schedules. To make matters worse, my roommate was a friend of the previous commander who was relieved because of my sexual harassment case against him. I could not escape her snide remarks. She was in contact with him, would talk to me about him and then stop in mid-sentence and remark about the situation. I tried to explain my side. I requested that she stay out of it because it did not concern her, but her behavior didn't change.

Email home January 5th, 2006

> *I hear much of the violence going on around here and it is an everyday occurrence. There are mortar attacks and often you will hear a missile. Today I heard about nine explosions and several of them were large weapons. It is a weird feeling being around explosions knowing that they are close and most of them are doing harm to someone or something. I moved into a trailer with a roommate. I have to walk a distance to get to the bathroom and I hope I can adjust to it. It is cold here so it is difficult to walk to the bathroom at night or when it is so cold.*

More sounds and hazards were introduced when I moved into the trailer. I lived near a helicopter pad and they flew above us 24 hours a day. It shook like there was an earthquake and the smell of their fuel lingered in the air. Likewise, mortars, gun shots and loud booms were the norm. Flares often fell from the helicopters and startlingly landed on top of our trailers. The Iraqis shoot their guns in the air frequently and stray bullets would fly through the air and often land on our trailers. I know we in the United States shoot guns in the air during New Year's Eve celebrations and that is dangerous enough, but this happened quite often and did not feel the same.

My fight or flight instinct was activated when I arrived in Iraq. It feels like a button is turned on, set to high and never turned off. I remained hyper-vigilant and always ready. I rarely slept the whole year I was in Iraq, but the first month in particular set the tone for the coming months.

Every day I listened on edge for mortars and rockets, waiting for one of them to land on or near me.

After a few weeks I moved into my own hooch. I finally had some privacy and was relieved to be away from my previous roommate. Though I was by myself, the all-white trailers have thin fake wood walls. I could hear my neighbors all the time, especially since we worked different schedules.

Email home January 21, 2006

> *I miss home tremendously. I miss everything about it. I don't drive anymore. I walk everywhere. I encourage all of you to try that for a day! I put on lots of miles in a week. We are still working 96 plus hours a week.*
>
> *I finally got my own space to live in. I had a roommate for the last 6 months. It is nice, but there are helicopters flying about 50 feet above our homes everyday 24 hours a day so not much rest for the weary.*
>
> *So the next time you feel the need to complain about anything . . . just remember that I and 130,000 of us are here in this madness. Oh you will say we joined and you signed up for it . . . I have heard all the arguments . . . I can only say that we did and we will continue to do it . . . it just is not easy to do.*

I finally caught the Kuwaiti crud. Being sick in Iraq was no fun. Taking "sick time" is not an option. Nobody brought me chicken soup or orange juice. No one visited me or cared that I was sick. I had a high fever and had no energy, but even with a high fever I still had to walk to the bathroom. It was a very difficult thing to do. When my fever broke, I awakened in a cold sweat and my bed was soaked. I needed to take a shower and clean myself up. It took everything within me to walk to the shower. It felt like it took me an hour to get to the shower trailer, take a quick shower and get back in bed because I was so weak.

31

Email home January 21, 2006

I am currently sick with what we all call here the "Kuwaiti crud". Basically it is an upper respiratory infection with vengeance. I got sick five days ago and began blowing gobs of dark yellow crap out of my nose and spent each morning and night coughing up a lung. I went to the MD and got Allegra and some antihistamines. It didn't work. I coughed more and had more yellow crap. I started antibiotics today in hopes of feeling better soon. So I talked to the doctor and he told me that most Americans get sick here because there is sand in the air and it contains microbes. I heard a rumor that some federal agency did a health study on soldiers in Iraq and found that we suffer from upper respiratory problems because Americans should not live in Iraq . . . HAHAHAHA. No shit Sherlock . . . . I could have told you that and not spent millions of dollars.

I also had a urinary tract infection. I couldn't understand it—I didn't get it from the more traditional way of complications following sex because I wasn't having sex in Iraq. I discovered it is a common problem for women because we hold our urine for long periods due to lack of bathroom facilities or lack of time. If there wasn't an available bathroom, many women urinated on themselves or found a place to go like in the sand or behind a building. Even after I was home for the first few years I held my urine. I got used to it and had to re-train myself to go to the bathroom.

I received so much support from my friend Greg whom I met in Fort Riley. While he was working in Balad, Iraq, he called and emailed me as much as he could. The first time he called me in January. I was shocked and happy to hear his familiar voice. We remained in touch, laughing about our crazy work situations and all the madness that was around us. A conversation with him always lifted my mood. It was nice to have a friend to talk to and I looked forward to his calls. He survived the Vietnam War and he was committed to having his unit members survive Iraq. I admire his dedication and respect his opinions. Most of all, he and I could talk and laugh with each other and that simple act of feeling connected in a war zone made a world of difference.

The first 90 days were an adjustment to war. Kuwait prepared us for the substandard living conditions: the dirty sand, filthy port-a-potties and walking a distance to take a shower and go to the bathroom. But in Iraq I was introduced to war. Overloaded with information, not sleeping, constantly anxious, and chaos filled my days. I was not sure how to cope in the environment and had to learn from those around me. Mortars would land close to our building and I would see the dust falling from the ceiling tiles, but no one moved or changed what they were doing. They worked and talked as if nothing happened. I wanted to get under the desk or to another safe place, but I learned, like the others, to continue to do what I was doing. The rule in Iraq was that if we heard the mortar it was good. To not hear them meant we were dead.

Work environment

I found out in Kuwait that I would not be working with my unit in the Media Operation Center. Instead, I worked in the Division's Public Affairs section. It was unclear exactly what I would be doing, but my first assignment was to develop an Arabic Media Assessment tool. My job was to compile Arabic media analysis sent from higher commands, search the internet for current Arabic media and analyze and compile information to be used by my superiors. I had no idea what I was doing, but I did my best.

In the beginning I didn't have a set schedule. I was overwhelmed: this large building was filled with chaos and anxiety. My work section was the same way. Information came at me fast and I had to learn as much as I could as quickly as possible. Communication was very difficult. I understood military speak, but war language was a whole new set of acronyms, meanings, terms and ideas. I often found myself looking at the person talking to me like a deer in a headlight. I carried a notebook with me to take notes and learn new terms. I had many skills to offer but needed time to learn where there was none.

In my first week my boss gave me a binder for the general's daily media update. He gave me headings to use, which I didn't understand. I asked him to interpret his handwriting for me. He scowled and told me I needed to get used to it. I tried for a while to decipher his headings, print tiny labels for dividers, answer phones and conduct a shift change briefing. After an hour and a half, I finally figured everything out and took the finished binder to him.

"Why did it take you over an hour to make this book?"

"Sir, I am not an administrative type; it took me a while, but—"

"Why aren't you an admin type?" he asked.

"Sir, at home I had a secretary who did the admin work," I said.

"What the fuck—a secretary?!" he turned to his office mate. "Did you hear that? She had a secretary. A fucking secretary. Really, that's hilarious. Well you are now the secretary, so you'd better get used to it."

As I walked away, I could still hear him talking and laughing about "a secretary." He was mean and unprofessional. I knew that I was most likely being treated this way because I was a woman and a Reservist and that it was going to be a long year. I was working in an infantry division where there were a limited amount of women. Since I was a Reservist and in their minds, not a "real soldier," talking to me in this manner was justified.

For the next few days the active duty members of my section continued to be non-communicative, vague and very disrespectful. I often stood up for myself and my soldiers, and complained to my commander about the unprofessional and hostile environment. After the third week a meeting was held to try to improve our working relationships. During the meeting we were incorrectly referred to again as the "United States Army Reserves National Guard" instead of our proper title. I was at war, living in hell with a group of people who didn't like Reservists and had no idea how to deal with us. The meeting was unproductive and I realized it was never going to change.

War is a 24-hour operation: the enemy never sleeps, so neither did we. It would have been easier if we got along with the people we worked with, but for some reason it was one of the most difficult things to do. It takes time to build a team and get to know each other. In more normal circumstances people have time, but during war there is a quick turn around and people are under extreme pressure. We had a huge mission, our work never stopped and it was important to work as a team.

It took me about a month to be able to navigate my work environment. Hostility came from the people I worked with in addition to the war itself. I never looked forward to going into work. People were always yelling at each other, calling each other "dumb ass," disrespected, humiliated and stressed out. The pressure was high to succeed and not make a mistake. There was war outside and a war within each section. The disunity between soldiers amazed me. I've worked in some bad work environments, but none as chaotic, hostile and disrespectful as the military while in Iraq.

Email home March 16, 2006

> *The active duty component does not treat the reserve soldiers with any amount of respect and consider us "hired hands." I overheard a conversation here from senior leaders saying, "The reservist should take their whiny assess and all their toys and go home." I am in paradise here. Not wanted or liked and a woman too. Odds are against me here.*

Mortars landed all around our area and they hit closer and closer to where I worked and slept. I lived in the area they called "mortar alley". It was a big hill with red flashing lights that made perfect targets for mortars and rockets. So as the enemy began to get better at their craft they were able to get closer to hitting an area where people lived and worked. There were many days when I would walk across mortar alley and hope that a mortar wouldn't land while I was in the area. It was a chance I took. In February mortars landed so close to my living area that it scared me to my core.

Email home February 18, 2006

> *Today was the closest we have come to being hit by mortars. In fact, they were so close they shook my trailer and got me running to figure out what just had happened and who was hurt and what I could do. Let me explain my day. I went to sleep at 9:30 am. I work nights and I was dead asleep and around 3 o'clock I heard digging around my trailer. Now many of you may not understand my concern about digging, but you see that is how Iraqis bury IED's. So I look out my window and all I see is an Iraqi man using a pick axe digging a trench between my trailer and another and burying a red wire. I don't see their faces and they are whispering and speaking Arabic. We have been trained to identify IEDs and all the activities that these men were performing rang a bell and I was scared. I grabbed my weapon and put it in the ready position and I went out to*

confront them. I had my Scooby Doo pajama bottoms on, pink flip flops and my M16. To my surprise they were just putting up a satellite dish, hence the digging and the wires. Still it got my blood pumping. I ended up going back to sleep eventually and around 8:30 pm I was awakened by mortars being launched. Not many people know what that sounds like, but once you hear it you know what happens next. I sat straight up in my bed. By now it is pitch black and I heard four loud booms and they are close and my trailer continues to shake. I jump up and put on my Army sweat pants, I grab my Army jacket and put on my pink flip flops and run outside. It is dark and I hear people screaming in the background, calling out to find out what just happened and where did the mortars hit. I go running in the dark, not sure where or why. I felt helpless. I go around the corner and I see soldiers running and I ask them what happened. They say we were mortared and it was close. How close I ask and they say by the Morale and Welfare Recreation (MWR) tent. That tent was probably 400-600 feet away from my trailer. Very close. I stop and try to figure out what to do. By now it is silent and everyone seemed to have returned back to their hootches. I hear helicopters flying to the areas to respond to the place where the mortars came from. I wait for gunfire to take place, nothing. The terrorist are long gone. I am in a state of shock I try to process what just happened. I finally calm down and take a shower and I meet a girl in the bathroom and she tells me that her roommate and several others freaked out and are still upset. I told her I understood, but still I did not realize the impact it would have on me . . .

We are fighting an enemy we can't see. I ran into the dark with my weapon ready to do something, yet I could not see or hear anything. What was I going to do you ask? I have no idea. It was instinct, it was survival. It was something. That is the reality of Iraq. We are in the dark trying to bring light to a nation who refuse to come into the light, they prefer the dark. I could not see anything, except watch the black smoke rise above our housing area and smelled a metal smell after something blows up. The impact of tonight will go much deeper in my being. For now I am scared. I did not know how I would react to these events because they do happen all the time, but in a distance from where I am. This was too close for comfort and it is hard to deal with. I am alive and no one was injured or killed That is something I am grateful for. Everyone says if you hear the mortar than you are fine. It is the ones you don't, well then that is not good, if you know what I mean.

All I can say is that all that little shit you are worried about and all the drama with friends and family can cease at any time. What matters is living, loving and laughing. We are all so important.

In February, I made some calls home. I was able to get in touch with my dad. I talked to him about what I was doing and described my work environment. I told him that I felt like I was a little fish in a shark tank and it was getting harder and harder to stay ahead. I didn't know that there were two people in the other section present who heard my conversation. When I hung up the phone, two people walked out of their cubicles and approached me and started joking with me. They nicknamed me Nemo. My father advised me to find my purpose. I set out to find something I could do that would bring me a sense of worth. Two days after I got the nickname, I found a Nemo toy sitting on my desk. It made me smile. I put it on my shelf to remind me I did not have to change who I was. But I did change eventually. War required us to change in order to survive mentally and emotionally.

I learned that there were many forward operating bases (FOB) that didn't have a Post Exchange (PX) or any real support on getting items. I was one of the lucky ones because I got care packages every week. Friends and family sent me anything and everything they could: cookies, candy, toiletries, cards and pictures. I always shared with my section and donated goodies to the Chaplain so he could take them to soldiers who received nothing. Sadly, there were many who never received packages or letters. I organized a toiletry drive and my friends and family came through for me again. My friend Leeann in California had her daughter's Girl Scout troop donate large boxes of Girl Scout cookies and toiletries. They also drew pictures and made cards. Thirty-six boxes were mailed to me and I got them to the Chaplain to distribute to those who needed them the most. Even during war I wanted to help others. I needed to do something to keep myself alive inside, to hold onto my compassion for others. That is how I found my purpose. I wanted and needed to help those who needed help. So soldiers in need were what I focused on.

Email home March 6, 2006

> *I miss home and miss all of you. I am grateful for all the boxes and cards and especially for those who sent items to soldiers that needed them. It is a shame that not all soldiers get what they need for survival and I am glad many of you stepped up to the plate and did something about it. I thank you for your help.*

In March I had been following a story about U.S. units being mortared and shot at from a remote area in the desert. Every time units investigated they found nothing but mortar rounds and other military equipment. Soldiers eventually located the source: the perpetrators were fellow Americans. These "Americans" were arrested for committing terrorist's acts against their own. I was confused and profoundly saddened by this. It seemed to me that as soon as the United States and other nations came to Iraq, everyone who wanted to kill or get in the action came as well.

Introduction to the civilian media

Having civilian news reporters embedding with units was another reason to worry. Some reporters were used to war conditions and knew the consequences but there were many who weren't. Reporters from various television, newspapers, radio and other forms of media wanted to embed and go to the areas with the most action. Any media that wanted to be embedded in units in Iraq had to be credentialed and understand the dangers of war. The process was tedious and detailed.

No one could come into the battle space without approval so much to our surprise, Jill Carroll, a reporter from the *Christian Science Monitor*, was kidnapped. Since she was not registered or credentialed under the United States, she was not protected by military forces. Her kidnapping was surprising and very confusing. She had been in Iraq since 2003 working as an independent reporter and lived with the Iraqis. Orders were directed to begin search and rescue missions for her. Hundreds of soldiers spent countless days and nights searching for her. The U.S. was using significant resources to find her. It became a cat and mouse game, and I watched many rescue attempts only to find she had been moved to another location. It was frustrating to say the least. The kidnappers took videos of her with demands on what needed to be done for her release. Our forces searched high and low for her. It was looking quite bleak.

As soldiers continued to look for Jill Carroll, another incident occurred with a high profile media correspondent. Bob Woodruff, an anchor from ABC, was critically injured by an IED explosion while working on a story with U.S. and Iraqi soldiers. While driving down a road, an IED exploded and severely injured Bob and his cameraman. U.S. soldiers saved their lives. Their medical skills and their ability to act in a crisis were amazing. I was so proud of those soldiers who helped Bob and his cameraman. This incident made its way to the President and it changed that way media conducted their operations in a war zone. I learned first-hand the dangers the civilian media would encounter while in Iraq. When I became the Media Embed Coordinator in July, I took safety precautions and procedures seriously. If reporters violated the rules, they were not allowed to work in our battle space or would get sent back to the United States.

In February, the Samarra mosque was bombed and the gold dome destroyed. This was a major problem for the U.S. and our allies and a significant disruption in Iraq. Sectarian violence erupted throughout the region. I was on duty during the chaos. The Arabic media reported that the United States military intentionally bombed the mosque. Since Saddam's capture the country was without a government, and life in Iraq was unstable. Violence erupted all over Iraq and I personally believe it was the start of the civil war. Fighting and killing was targeted at the Iraqis but also the U.S. and our allies. We had to act quickly—every section in division went into crisis mode. As more information was gathered and details unfolded, we learned that Iraqis were hiding bombs, mortars and other weapons in the basement of the mosque and blew it up themselves. I don't know whether it was intentional or unintentional but the U.S. had nothing to do with it.

As a public affairs officer, I learned very quickly how the Iraqi media and terrorists operated. They could spin a story quickly and turn the whole country against the United States and our allies. I monitored the Arabic media, learning more and more about our enemy. Despite how I may have felt about their politics or religion, I knew that we (psychological operations, public affairs and other sections) needed to step up our game to counter all the negative media being generated. I was on board with the war effort. I now understood war language and was immersed in it. I felt like I had given my soul to the dark side.

Email home February 27th, 2006

> *I am still working long hours and no days off. I am tired and weary. Your mind plays tricks on you when you are exhausted, believe me. I miss home so much. I really feel like I have been forgotten in many ways. Don't get me wrong I know I am loved and miss everyone so much, but I am also missing everything, the little things matter to me. The nights out with the girls, what is happening with the latest in people's lives, with everything? No offense to any of my family or friends. I am just expressing my feelings here. I am in a foreign country that is hostile, in a civil war and bombing the shit out of us daily, with people I don't know and minimal support. We lost three soldiers in the last 48 hours, 2 by roadside bomb and one was killed by direct fire, I unfortunately watched the video of the soldier being shot. A group of people were watching the video for analysis. It puts a damper on how you feel about what is going on here. I do believe in everything I am doing, it is a heavy burden to bear.*

In March, Jill Carroll, the reporter from the *Christian Science Monitor*, was released unharmed. She walked into an Iraqi political office and asked for help. American soldiers were called to the site and eventually sent her home. Before she left, a video of Ms. Carroll criticizing the occupation of Iraq and praising the insurgents as "good people fighting an honorable fight" appeared on an Islamist website. I witnessed all of her rescue operation attempts, each time on the edge of my seat hoping that they would rescue her alive. Her negative statement towards the U.S. and the U.S. military outraged me. I really don't think she or anyone else knew about the efforts that brave men and women put in to find and rescue her. It was reported that she was forced to say these things, but regardless, it was an outrage. I was involved 100 percent with this rescue. I may not have been actually doing the rescue missions, but I was there and when she made that statement I felt nothing but rage.

A New Job

The night shift public affairs battle captain was fired and I was selected to work in the position. I worked 8 p.m. to 8 a.m. and it was a tough shift to work. I had to change my natural sleep pattern while adding the pressure of working during the busiest time. Combat operations happen at night. The person who was fired was always screamed at, and it was not a position I wanted to be in.

I worked very hard at this job. It was busy and I had numerous responsibilities: I supervised four personnel and each had their own responsibilities that ultimately helped me at my job. I monitored intense combat operations. The things I witnessed while doing this job were often overwhelming and very upsetting. I witnessed combat operations being conducted on a large screen via satellite.

My first vivid image of death took place during my second day on this assignment. This particular event really made an impact on me. I watched the combat operation taking place on the large screen when I heard and saw an IED explosion. Some soldiers were thrown out of their vehicles; others were running and screaming over the radio for help. On the screen I watched a soldier, someone's son, maybe husband or a father, burn alive. People tried to save him, but they were under attack. He died a horrible death and I was absolutely helpless to do anything.

Though I was powerless to help him, my adrenaline was running as if I was trying to. I looked around and everyone continued to work as usual. They observed this incident and made the reports without any acknowledgment of what just happened. I began to cry. I made eye contact with a man who I worked with and he walked over to me. I just shook my head and whispered to him, "Let's say a prayer for them." We bowed our head in prayer and then went back to work. I watched others die in combat attacks and it never got easier for me. When these horrible events took place, I completed my tasks and then left on my break and cry. I cried for the person who died and their loved ones. I cried for myself because I felt so alone and so afraid. At times I asked myself if I reacted this way because I was weak. I now know that I am human. I witnessed so many people trying to be something other than human and watched them fail miserably. They may have masked their feelings but they took their own sadness, fear and anger out on others. Since I was a woman and a Reservist, I was the perfect target.

Email home May 16, 2006

Last month over 60 U.S. soldiers were killed by IED's. This month we are starting out with a new record high and it is on the 7th of May. It gets harder to hear the news. We are living it here, so I can only imagine the over saturation at home and the inability to remain attentive to it, I even find it harder and harder to remain focused and motivated. I have worked some shitty jobs and with some horrible people, but this takes the cake. Believe me, I can tell you when you all are having a bad day or your co-worker is acting crazy or your boss is acting nuts . . . well I am certain that your boss did not kick a box of water across the room and scream and almost have a heart attack over someone not being at their desk, or no one called you "fucking stupid," so remember on your worst day it is better than most of ours. I may be getting off night shift soon and maybe out of this department. Please pray for that to happen soon. I would be happy to just have a "normal" schedule. We are losing soldiers here daily and it gets harder and harder to come into work. War is hell for everyone involved. I know people back home are sick of this and believe me I think so are the soldiers, they might be questioning the "why of it all"? The Iraqi people voted in December and it is now May and still no government. Unbelievable violence is committed against each other by their own kind. As we move into the future with all our technology and future thinking here it is nowhere to be found. It seems their culture is founded on violence and it is promoted. This is a place where lying is an accepted practice. We (U.S) are working with the Iraqi security forces and many times we show up for operations and they don't, or they inform the "bad guys" we're coming so they move to another location. How can you defeat the enemy when the enemy already knows your moves?

I got the most disgusting email a few days ago. It was a video clip attached of an American woman talking about why soldiers should be killed by IEDs and used the bible to justify it. As I watched my blood boiled and then I realized that we, military men and women, who will fight and defend our country at home and abroad, allow for her to say those things, though she does not even know or understand that. She uses God to justify death. I may not be the most religious person, but I believe in a God as a loving God and not one who purposefully sets out to harm another. And I hear the saga still continues with the church people protesting soldiers' funerals. My heart is so saddened by this. I can't imagine being hit by an IED and the pain it would cause before one dies.

I decided to try something nice for people I was working with. We were always busy and most people around me had no idea what was happening at home. We had a system that could communicate with via voice of internet, and I decided to create a small in-house radio show. I picked out the top ten news reports and entertainment news from home and read the script to let people around me know what was happening. Some nights there were five people and others nights I had thirty. I gave it a good run, but the Iraqis finally elected their government and my radio show came to a halt.

Email home May 20, 2006

The Iraqis elected their government; history itself has been made. It was an uneventful day, not a lot of violence and it seemed to be quiet. We will wait to see what happens tomorrow. Let's hope that the Iraq government can take control over their country and let the rest of us go back to ours. It seems like there is so much going on back home that needs to be taken care of. I will stop for now and get this sent to you . . . know that I love and miss all of you.

One of my primary responsibilities was to gather all the necessary information and put together the general's media binder. It was always a struggle to meet the 5:45 a.m. deadline. There was always something happening that was more pressing or more important, but I managed to get it done. One morning around 5:30 a.m. I was at the copy machine and a higher ranking officer needed to make a copy. He didn't say anything to me; he just paced around me and the machine. While copies were coming out of the machine, I stepped aside to place some of the papers into the binder. He stopped my copy job to make his copy. I explained to him that I had less than five minutes to get the general's binder and his staff binders to them and I was on a short deadline. The officer got very angry, pulled his copy out of the machine, kicked the copy machine and screamed "fuck!" before storming off. I was dumbfounded. There were several other copy machines in the area that were not being used. Incidents like this happened all the time. Surviving the daily outbursts and irrational behavior became the norm. The culture was set up this way and since I was in the culture, I found myself acting in similar ways. I would yell about coffee not being made or too much trash in the trash can. It was stupid, irrelevant stuff. Irrational behavior was accepted but internally I knew that this wasn't who I was. I had to renew my faith in myself and others and remember who I was.

We had a designated U.S. phone in our section and the number was distributed to soldiers and their families in the U.S. to call our office for information. Because there is a nine-hour time difference, the phone usually rang at night when I was on duty. Many calls were from family members who wanted to know if their loved one was killed or injured. That information was not to be given out. Even though I did know who was killed or wounded that day, I couldn't tell the person on the phone. The standard line that we were instructed to use was, "I am not allowed to give out that information at this time." I could hear the desperation in the callers' voices. It bothered me so much, but I followed the rules and only disclosed what I was allowed to. One night a father of a soldier called the phone number about 5 times, every 2 hours. I gave him the standard line and he sighed and began to cry. I had to tell him the same thing over and over. It tore at my heart. I knew his son was alive, but couldn't say anything.

When the day shift supervisor arrived, I described how hard it is to talk to distraught family members and asked if there was another way I could get them information. He compromised by allowing us to say that the Army would notify them within 24 hours of death or injury, so if it was past 24 hours they had their answer. The father called me shortly after we developed the new protocol. He desperately asked once again if I knew if his son was killed. I told him if he had not been notified within 24 hours of the incident, he had his answer. For about 30 seconds there was silence, and then he spoke. He told me it had been past 24 hours and that his son had to be alive. I could hear relief in his voice. Soldiers are someone's child, parent, spouse, partner, cousin, aunt, nephew or dear friend. We are people and many people love us. I imagined my family and how desperate they must of felt, watching the news and wondering what was happening to me. He thanked me. I told him that he would hear from his son and to get some rest. I was glad to do something meaningful for someone else. I am sure I will never meet him or his son, but I know that he was at peace because his son was alive and that was all he wanted to know. Helping develop the protocol may not have been my biggest accomplishment during deployment, but it certainly brought compassion to others.

When a soldier is killed, the military has 24 hours to notify the next of kin. The body is flown back to the United States. Casualty Notification Officers get the call with as many details and are sent to the soldier's home to notify the family about the death of their son or daughter. They have twenty-four hours from the death to notify the family. The system is not without faults or problems, but it usually works. Since we are technologically advanced and there is access to the internet, email, Facebook, etc., there were times when people found out via social media or an email that their loved one was dead. So to mitigate those circumstances many bases cut off internet access until the family was notified by the Casualty Notification Officer.

Email home May 25, 2006

> *Things here are the same. So much violence. People die in large numbers every day. It is very sad. I guess you heard about the pregnant lady being killed. Just know that it was not intentional like the media wishes to think. They were driving towards a checkpoint, there are signs everywhere telling them what to do etc. It was a restricted area and well unfortunately it happened. I know in my heart they did not shoot to kill, but it is being made out to be an intentional act. Maybe the Iraqis will get sick of us being here and ask us to go home, we should really . . . this is their country and we have done enough. They have a government and they have security forces. It is time for them to take the lead and take care of their own. They say 18 mos. before we go . . . . I hope so . . . .*

There is talk of war crimes committed here by Marines and soldiers. I do not know who is right or wrong. Soldiers die daily here, get shot at and we are doing everything we can to do the right thing. I was not in Haditha and I cannot say they did or did not do what is being claimed, but I can tell you the truth is always somewhere in the middle. If you see the poor Iraqis on TV the story they told that reporter is not the same one they told the other one before. It is customary here to lie outright and have no shame in their game. I don't want to take sides either. I am just saying the truth is in the middle.

The government cannot do anything about this violence because they do not have the nominees for their top security positions. No one is leading the army or police. It is willy nilly here. Corruption and sectarian lines keep many people from those positions. It is difficult to find someone that would not be corrupt or have ties to Iran. Iran is just sitting in the back waiting for their turn. We will leave and Iran and Iraq will be united, not so willingly but they are patient and will take this country as soon as they can. All our work will go back to the dictatorship. That is all these people know. Friends, my heart bleeds and is filled with sorrow for the Iraqi people, but it is not as rosy as we want it to be. The U.S. has done wonderful things here and provided help in many areas. But it has not changed anything. The insurgents are still killing hundreds of people a day, kidnapping, sabotaging the oil pipe lines and destroying anything that is good for the people. I think the American people have reached their maximum capacity for this, yet nothing is done. Politicians' talk is cheap . . . It seems like everyone knows more about what is going on here and they have never been here. Also there is the whole political realm that people can't tell the truth or they will lose their jobs, I have seen it with several generals in the past here. They have lost their jobs and found retirement because they told the truth. It is sad to know that the truth is no longer accepted and we must lie in order to maintain our positions of power. Maybe somebody could change the government and put ethics and the truth back in. That the truth about Iraq is that it is a dead issue. If there is hope, it will come after we are gone. When we do what soldiers do we get into trouble. Iraqis kill and torture each other every day . . . a day does not go by unharmed. Their houses are mortared; they are snatched out of their beds and blind folded and taken to a field and executed daily . . . Please do not misunderstand me, I am not saying soldiers are justified in killing people—it is all based on the situation. But this is a violent society, one in which we cannot or will not understand. Since I watch all of this violence happen, I have an opinion worth considering . . .

Some other news: I will be meeting with my commander to discuss what I am supposed to do next; hopefully it will be not on nights. The people I met here are awesome and help me through the crazy. I am glad to have made friends and have some outlet. Also I want to tell all of you, thanks for your support. I know I am a lucky gal to have you in my life. The small things matter . . . I do appreciate it all.

We have made our 6 month mark so hopefully time will go by and November will be here in no time . . .

Working the night shift as the Battle Captain took its toll on me in an unexpected way. I could feel my anger rise towards the Iraqis yet my heart broke for them. They lived under a horrible dictatorship. Many were living in poverty with limited or no electricity and raw sewage and trash everywhere. Freedom of speech was non-existent; speaking out against the government resulted in prison or death. Moreover, their media was completely censored so the information they received was corrupted or distorted. They were trapped in the dark ages by no fault of their own. There seems to be little difference between the way modern day Iraqis live and medieval Europe. All of this weighed conversely in my mind with my rage against them for killing my fellow soldiers. Many Iraqi intellectuals who desperately wanted a democracy had already fled the country, so we were stuck with the Iraqis who could not escape or didn't want to. One day, certain Iraqi tribal leaders were our allies and the next day they were our enemies. Many Iraqis could not be trusted. I deplore prejudice in all of its forms but I developed a prejudice against these people because my life and the life of our soldiers depended on being cautious of them. It was a slippery slope to hate and I grappled with myself internally.

During one of my night shifts, two U.S. Army soldiers were kidnapped. I watched the video of them being kidnapped and was alongside the immediate rally to search for these soldiers. Their fellow soldiers searched day and night, without sleep or taking time to eat. The search continued for days. As a result of the kidnapping, monitoring of terrorists websites increased. Several days after the kidnapping, the terrorist group responsible posted a video depicting the torture and murder of these 2 soldiers. The section's supervisor was not available, so a soldier contacted me to show me the video for verification purposes. I was one of the first people to view this video and verify that it was who we were looking for. Since it was evening most of the leadership was gone for the day, so I had direct orders to wake my boss and the general to review the video. As I ran towards my boss' trailer, I suddenly felt violently ill and I began throwing up. I couldn't linger, so I wiped the vomit off my face and kept moving. I woke everyone and we began processing the video for analysis and terrain recognition. The next day our forces found the soldiers in an open area. Their bodies were badly burned and they were strapped with IEDs. I watched the recovery team pull them from the field. I sat in absolute dismay; I was witnessing senseless killing and torture of someone's loved one. Anger towards the Iraqis was rising.

More hazards

My 12-hour night shifts often turned into fourteen or sixteen hours and didn't allow much time for anything else. I had to choose between eating, sleeping or showering on a daily basis. One new twist to showering was a group of women who lingered in the shower trailer to get glimpses of naked women. I have never cared about anyone's sexual orientation. I also know that most lesbians don't behave this way. I believe that gay, lesbian and bisexual men and women should be allowed to serve openly in the military, without discrimination. But after a 16-hour day in the hell hole I worked in and after not taking a shower for a few days, a nice quiet shower, in privacy, without being ogled was all I wanted. There were many days when I would just look in the shower trailer and if anyone was in there, I kept walking.

As a woman in a war zone I was very aware of the possibility of being raped. It happened, probably more than what I heard about. I took every precaution. I made friends with several people I worked with and one of them would always meet me at my hooch to walk me to work, midnight chow. I always tried to have someone with me. If I didn't have someone to accompany me, I would put my magazine in my weapon and walked in the ready position. If anyone came near me I would have shot them. It was very dark in Iraq. There are no lights, and if the moon is waning or the stars are not bright, you can't see your hand in front of your face. One night my friend was late coming by to pick me up, so I decided to walk on my own. I had my M16 in the ready position, my finger on the selector switch and the magazine loaded. I could lock and load my weapon in a second. It was very dark, but out of the corner of my eye I saw a shadow moving on the other side of the trailers. We walked side by side about 15 feet apart with the trailers as the dividers, but when I got to the last trailer the shadow was gone. Suddenly I saw a silhouette coming towards me. I lifted my M16 and I yelled, "I don't know who you are and why you are following me, but I am about to shoot you." The silhouette stopped and yelled, "Michelle, it's me, I was coming back to walk you to work." I cut him off and said "okay, good thing you spoke." We laughed and kept on walking. He told me he was glad I didn't shoot first and then ask questions.

On the sidelines . . .

I had to deal with rumors, gossip, jealousy, envy and "one uppers." I was amazed that people behaved this way while at war where fellow soldiers were dying and suffering. I did my best to avoid drama but at times I was drawn in. If you were a woman, rumors ran wild with accusations of sleeping with male soldiers. If you talked to a male for "too long," smiled or were nice, it was rumored that you were having sex with him. "See how she talks to him, they must be having sex." Marriages and relationships were ruined by rumors. Rumors hurt feelings and working relationships. Both men and women started the rumors and kept them going. While I had sex with no one, I was accused of sleeping around. It was worse than being in high school. Women should bond with each other in the military. But some turned against one another. When war is mixed with hundreds of men and a lot of testosterone, some women become competitors instead of allies.

A female captain moved into the trailer next to me and we began talking and having lunch when we could. So I was accused of being a lesbian by another female officer in my unit. It seemed like every other week I was being addressed by my commander about some lie this same officer told him. Her antics wore me out to the point where it became funny in a very ridiculous way. I got so tired of her harassment that in July I went to file a formal harassment complaint against her. I didn't file it, but began the process. I explained to my commander that I had enough and that if he couldn't control her, I would do what I needed to do because her behavior was more than ridiculous. I began documenting the nonsense and agreed to meet with my commander to get it resolved.

July 6, 2006 2100 hours

> *I met with commander at 1900 hours to go over my performance counseling. We discussed the current status of CPT #### and what was going to be done. He explained to me what his plan was. If I experienced further harassment from her or I heard any more rumors to inform him immediately. His words were very direct and honest. He told me that she is focused on me and looking for ways to get me. I am giving him the opportunity to handle the issue as my commander, but if anything else happens, I will inform him and go to EO and make a complaint. I began journaling the events, her statements and actions and am willing and able to forward with this complaint.*

The sexual harassment case continues

While I was in Iraq my previous commander was given an "Article 15" and decided to challenge it. This required me to testify in court. I would either have to go home to testify or do so via teleconference. It was very upsetting to say the least. I wondered how much longer I would have to endure this. I did not have anyone in the military to share this with. Once again I talked to the chaplain but it didn't seem to help. I was in the middle of a war zone, plagued with rumors, with little support and I had to survive the madness that I was in the middle of. Fortunately, I didn't have to testify again. He received his Article 15 and lost his Active Guard Reserve job because of the overwhelming amount of evidence against him. Just like most perpetrators, he continued to claim his "innocence," rallied his supporters and portrayed me as the "bad guy."

There were only a few ways to work off stress. My way was to work out and run, despite the risks of being hit by a mortar round. The "crew," the group of friends I made during my night shift, made a pact that we had to work out before each meal and run at least 2-4 miles per week as our schedules allowed. If I missed a day or two, it negatively impacted the way I felt. I met other runners and we formed a running group. We ran at our dinner break a few days a week. There were many days when a mortar landed in the distance while we ran and we just continued to run. We got used to war and all its noises. When I was running, I didn't care. I just wanted to run because it was the only time I felt free.

My third job

In July 2006, I became the Media Embed Coordinator for the division. My role was to coordinate national and international journalist into our battle space and highlight the good our soldiers and other service members and allies were doing. The one skill set I brought to the table was my ability to work with civilian media. I understood that building good relationships with the media made a world a difference.

I was already familiar with this job because I worked closely with the previous Embed Coordinator. I just needed to learn the correct procedures and protocol. There wasn't a lot of training time, and my hours changed again. There wasn't a set schedule; I worked day hours, night hours and early morning hours. The civilian reporters were busy and active at all time. Coordinating logistics for the media was a full time job. It is not easy moving around a war zone. Most of the time reporters/journalist would fly via helicopter to various areas around Iraq. Someone from the unit they were embedding with was responsible for picking them up and getting them to their areas. I coordinated their flight dates and times and made housing and transportation arrangements while they were in transit to their assignments and made sure they had meals while they worked. I met some amazing and wonderful reporters and journalist. Lara Logan, Richard Engel, Arwa Damon and photojournalist Yuri Kozyrev were some of the people I enjoyed a good working rapport with. I worked closely with them to get them where they needed to be, enabling them to get their stories and photos. They were grateful for all the hard work we did which allowed them to do their jobs.

But there were other reporters who weren't sensitive to the fact that we were in a war zone. There were a few reporters from FOX News who expected to be treated like royalty. They complained about everything, including their working conditions, their living quarters and the food. I wish I could name names. All I can say is that we (military men and women) lived and worked in the same conditions and made the best of our situation. One particular reporter was especially difficult to work with. I received a phone call around 1:00 a.m. requesting that I bring her food. She was disgusted with her evening meal and had no transportation to go anywhere. At 2:00 a.m. I put a bunch of granola bars in a bag with a Gatorade and drove to her living quarters. When I handed her the bag, she screamed that this was unacceptable. With a deadpan expression I told her, "If you don't like it here, please leave. I can get you on the next helicopter out of here. I will pick you up at 6 a.m. Be ready to go back to Baghdad where you can get a flight back to the U.S. You won't have to suffer anymore." She didn't respond. I showed up at 6 a.m. and she had changed her tune. She apologized for her rudeness and wanted to continue her assignment. She was the first reporter I wanted to throw out of the country and she wouldn't be the last.

Email home July 20, 2006

So here it is already July . . . I go on leave in 28 days . . . it could not come any quicker. So let's see what I have been up to.

July 4th was good in a way . . . not like home by any means, but what made it special was I was able to see the Space Station flying through the sky at 10:00pm our time. The Army has "space people" and they track all kinds of stuff so I got to go outside and watch it zoom through the air. It would never really happen at home; too much pollution and you have to be at the right place at the right time. I attempted to see the space station and the shuttle when they linked up after that, but seemed to miss the exact times. It was certainly amazing and it may have been a once in a lifetime event. I can't imagine flying around the world and seeing it from way up there. I guess it is like looking at the ocean which is endless and depthless and you see and feel how much power it has. Space may be something like that. Things here in Iraq are getting worse. There are large attacks against people and it is all sectarian violence. Civil war is what it is called, yet no one wants to call it as they see it. We live in a politically charged world, where no one has the guts to say what is really happening. Most people worry about their careers and not the truth. I have met some soldiers here that face death daily and they are questioning the reasons of why we are here. The Marines and Navy and Air Force all have the right idea, 6 month tours. It is the best time to move out; you miss the burn out and can leave without being jaded and angry. I think that is why I have stopped writing so often. I have no reason in my personal life to complain, I have wonderful friends and family members and I want for nothing here. Yet here I have found myself in anger and really frustrated. I have no support from anyone in my unit, I trust no one and so I rely on some others, whom are decent people whom I call friends. I feel I have changed and it may not be for the good. I have taken way too much shit from many people here and I have sat back and hoped that one day someone would assist me in the process; no one has the guts to step forward. I thank all my family and friends whom have taught me how to be a good person and I know that being a good person inside and out opens you up to be a target for those whom are miserable. It is tough here guys, believe me.

On a good note . . . I got to go on a 4 day pass for some much needed R&R and it was nice to get away and just be. I got to wear civilian clothes, swim and eat good food with taste. Most things here have no taste or taste the same. But anyway it was good to get away and just relax, actually think and sleep. I slept as much as I could, but I will never catch up here, when I get home I will become sleeping beauty, but of course a Starbucks coffee would wake me up. The pool there was awesome. The funny thing is that we arrived late at night on Thursday and just got a tour of the area and we turned in our weapons and all our gear. So Friday morning around 730 I heard massive gun fire and it was really close. I was worried and wondered why we turned our stuff in when we were so close to "action" the gunfire lasted for hours. At 1pm we had a briefing and they explained that it was a range. Though we were in a dangerous area and heard gunfire and explosions all the time and ambulances . . . it was sort of restful, but we never really relaxed. For me it was another surreal moment. We all laughed but knew we were in a bad area. I swam every day and lay in the sun, with gunfire in the background. Something you never get used to. It was in Baghdad, downtown and it was crazy. You never get away from the gunshots, the loud booms, but I was away from the chaos of my job and I did not have to work, but still it does not change where you are and the conditions you live in . . . I flew in a helicopter again, and this was at night over Baghdad. Let me tell you that they had lights, Baghdad was lit up with beautiful lights and every house had them. So when you hear Baghdad has no power don't believe the hype. It is very hot here, 124 degree is what the thermometer says, I know you guys are having some hot days too. It feels like a blow dryer that is on constantly, no relief anywhere. I am grateful for AC and shade. The sun is bright and it just seems to suck the life out of ya too. I heard you have 100's as well and I am sure there is humidity. We have no humidity and have had no rain since early May, it is hot and dry. It is the desert.

Big news on my end, due to the unbelievable nonsense here, I will be resigning my commission as an Officer in the United States Army Reserves as soon as I return home. It was a tough decision based on many factors, one includes never deploying again, and another is that I do not want to work with people who lack ethics, morals or the capability of having a thought of their own. I have learned many lessons here and this is the biggest decision I have made and it feels absolutely right. I know it is the correct decision because I can sleep better and god willing, the resignation will be approved and I will be done with this. I miss everyone madly and know that I am doing well. I am in a good place (I get to leave this place) and will be home in 4 months. The 1st Cav. Div. is replacing us . . . I have seen and met some of their people here, so I know they are coming . . . Keep praying for us. It is still incredibly violent here . . . The Middle East seems to have gone crazy. I will write you more . . .

In August I was injured. I heard a mortar round launched from its tube when walking to my job site. I ran towards a shelter while in full gear. As I was running, I slipped on some rocks and did a full split. I got up and continued to run. The mortar landed away from me, but it was too close for my comfort. Two days after this incident, I started feeling pain in my right upper leg near my hip and buttocks area. I went to the division doctor who gave me pain relievers and told me to rest my leg. It put a damper on my running, but I was still able to lift weights and continue my work out. I was fascinated that I didn't feel my injury right away. Our bodies' fight or flight instinct has a way of protecting us. After a few weeks of resting it, I got back to running. It was necessary for me to work out all of the negativity and stress.

Also in August a most unusual relationship formed. I never thought I would meet someone who would impact my life so significantly. I was working late and missed evening chow, so I went to another dining facility to grab a late dinner. The dining facility was pretty empty. I sat my tray on a table and walked away to get some water. When I returned a Colonel was sitting across from my tray. I hadn't seen him; I was thinking about work and knew I only had a short time to eat and get back. As awkward and embarrassed as I felt, he pleasantly requested that I sit down. The conversation was not typical of any I had with a person of his rank. We talked about life, work and home: a *normal* conversation. I actually felt like we could be friends if we weren't in this environment. We stayed in touch and eventually formed a friendship. Whenever we ran into each other, or had time, we talked. I was asked his advice and gave and received emotionally support. It was a bond I continue to have with him. It was never a romantic or sexual relationship. I believe we met each other because we both needed to find some way to be normal in an abnormal situation. I will be forever grateful to "G." I know in my heart that if I ever needed something or someone he would be there for me and I for him.

My rest and relaxation (R&R) could not come quickly enough. I finally got to go on leave in September. My boyfriend and I planned a trip to Greece and would be taking our R&R together. I was ready to get out of Iraq. I didn't want to come home because I was afraid I would not come back. It would have been too hard for me to say goodbye again. I enjoyed being in Greece and the reminder of the rest of the normal world.

Email home September 9, 2006

Hello All:

Most of you know by now that I went to Greece and visited Athens, Mykonos and saw many wonderful sights throughout. Greece is a beautiful place.

I woke up at 0400 on the 18th of Aug and headed to the airport here. I did not leave this place until 0300 on the 19th not having slept. We landed in Kuwait and waited to get the tickets issued. It was 150 degrees there. So I know it gets to be 104 at home, but never 150. 150 is hot as hell.

So it took me until the 21ˢᵗ of August to get to Athens. I slept for 16 hours at this little hotel called the Attalos. The view from the roof was that of the Acropolis.

I rode around on a motor bike. The island was very hilly and the houses are all white with blue doors. I went to Delos to visit the island that Artemis and Apollo were born. It was amazing to be on an island that was 4000 years old. History is amazing . . . I walked where the gods walked.

After the Acropolis, I rented a car and traveled throughout central Greece. Stopped at Thermopylae, which is home of a famous Spartan Battle, one that the military studies, but the important thing about it is that 300 Spartans and 700 hundred other Greek soldiers battled one million Persians. From Thermopylae went to Amfissa, a small mountain town and spent the night and just hung out. They had a community circle in the center of their town and it was so interesting to sit and watch the people. It was Sunday. Everything remained closed until 7 pm and then it all opened up and families old and young came to the center, to drink, to play and eat. Community at its best. It was nice to see. I took it all in and I miss the feeling of family and friends.

The next day drove to Delphi, which was my favorite place in many ways. It is the spot where the Oracle Delphi lived and told prophecies to the people and gods that came there. It was built on the side of the mountain. Ruins that archeologist are still uncovering. We think we are so advanced, but to see how they lived and the things they created, they were very advanced. Water ducts, heating elements for their homes and the necessary things to sustain a life. Pretty amazing. Got to see Hadrian's lover Antonios's statue. The Greeks do like their men.

I spent the night in Delphi, which the little mountain town reminded me of home in many ways. The shops and restaurants reminded me the central west end. I really felt good there. Unfortunately had to come back here, but I will never forget my trip to Greece. We have lots to do and catch up on. I am not seeing #### anymore, we broke up in Greece. But I can't focus on that now. I'm back in war . . . no time to think or no rest for weary. I love you and miss ya much and know I will be home soon.

Unfortunately my relationship with my boyfriend ended during my deployment. Having a relationship while deployed is very difficult. My boyfriend was stationed in the "Green Zone." He moved throughout Iraq and his job occasionally enabled him to stop by my area for lunch or dinner. But it was a far cry from a normal dating relationship. Both of us were always rushed and had to focus on our jobs. I introduced him to my friends. The "crew" was all males and we worked closely together. I had to form friendships in order to survive my work environment. Most of them were married with children. We talked about their wives and children and often shared our care packages with each other. Most of all we helped each other through some pretty awful times. My boyfriend met all of them and sometimes joined us for lunch. Soon he began making jealous remarks and requested that I stop spending time with them. I understood why he felt the way he did, but in reality I worked with all men and it was natural to form friendships with them. I explained that my friends and I maintained professional boundaries and were nothing more than friends. He continued to have issues with my relationships and it was a frequent topic of discussion or emails.

There were problems with this relationship from the beginning that I overlooked. I think I wanted to be in a relationship so badly that I settled. When I needed compassion and empathy from him, he gave me the same "hard line" crap I got from others around me. For instance, when a mortar landed near my hooch and I called him seeking comfort. Instead he told me to "buck the fuck up and get over it." I hung up on him. The one thing that kept me optimistic and motivated was our R&R trip to Greece together. I spent several days planning and gathering information. In my mind it was going to be the best trip ever. My family expected that during this trip that we would end up married. Secretly I wanted to get married in Greece. It seemed so romantic at the time. I thought that being married could make war tolerable.

Instead of getting married, the relationship ended in Greece. He was drunk all the time, disrespectful, and was frequently angry and argumentative. I couldn't wait for the fifteen days to end so I could get away from him. I knew couples often fought on R&R; it's part of deescalating from a war zone. I thought through good communication we would work it out. My dream of getting married ended, and I came back to reality and to war.

I only had two months left in country and I was anxious to get out of Iraq. I saw 1st Calvary patches walking around the building and it always brought a smile to my face. I knew our replacement would be coming soon. I just had to hang in there. I really enjoyed working as the media embed coordinator. It was a very demanding position, but it also gave me the opportunity to build good working relationships with many of the reporters from various networks. I was fascinated by their jobs and their work. I wanted to do a good job for them because deep down inside I wanted the media to cover our military men and women. If service men and women were on television, their families and friends at home would see them and know for that moment they were safe. So on those days when I was over worked, tired and hungry, I stayed focused and made sure I did whatever I could to get the reporters or photojournalist to their areas so they could tell the story. I built strong relationships with many of them, I trusted them and they trusted me.

Amid all of the craziness and chaos that accompanies a war zone, something very positive happened. In October a group organized a "Baghdad 10 Miler" race to coincide with the Army 10-miler at home. I always wanted to run the Army 10-miler held annually in Washington, D.C., but never had the opportunity. So I decided to run it in Iraq. The 10-mile course was laid out around our base with the last part of the race straight up "signal hill." This steep was not only grueling to run up but was also the hill that the enemy targeted with mortars and rockets. Running the "Baghdad 10 Miler" was a personal goal of mine. I was still healing from my injury, but when I ran the full ten miles I felt good and my leg didn't hurt until after the race. I don't remember my time, but I remember how proud I was of myself and all of us who finished the race.

We were wrapping up our time in Iraq. Our replacements were coming. I was getting more anxious about coming home. I had no place to live, no job, no boyfriend and saw all my future plans diminished. I started feeling trapped. I wanted to be excited and happy about leaving, but it was difficult because day after day things remained the same. War was always war, mortars continued to fall and work remain the same chaotic, depressing place.

Surge time

During the month of October U.S. forces geared up for surge operations in and around the Baghdad area. The surge was a major defensive/offensive strategy to quell violence around the area. The Brigade in the area where most of the operations would take place needed a Public Affairs Officer (PAO). I was selected as his replacement at the Brigade while operations were being conducted. I was unable to get transportation to the Brigade and no one wanted to assist me with this. My section didn't care how I got there but told me I had to go. All the helicopter flights were full and there was no room for me on the various convoys going to the area. I made every attempt to make arrangements to get to the Brigade. I had no other option but to ask the General's aide for assistance. I explained my dilemma to him and asked for help. His aide made arrangements for the General's Personal Security Detail (PSD) to take me.

That Sunday at 11:00 a.m. I was escorted to a line of vehicles, received my safety briefing and away we went. I was the only passenger in the vehicle and was taken to the Brigade. I was a 1st Lieutenant working in a Major's position. Best practices were never followed during my time working in Iraq. Rapport building, team building and common professional courtesy were never the norm. I had to fend for myself and never understood why it was always an uphill battle. People seemed to work so hard against each other. The surge waged on for some time and I witnessed amazing operations. The soldiers I worked with told stories about our brave men and their commitment to one another. *I wished I had that type of work environment.* After two weeks I headed back to my regular job. Time was ticking down but it never moved quickly enough. The men and women who worked "outside the wire" understood the value of teamwork. They relied on each other to stay alive, but the people I worked with never seemed to understand this concept.

October 21, 2006 email home

> *Hello. I have begun getting things tied up around here as we prepare to depart. We still don't know when, but I can't wait. It is busy here and it is the worst ever. I cannot wait to leave.*
>
> *I got some good or shall I say interesting news. I was offered a command of a unit back home. It is a captain's position and I may get promoted. They want me to stay in. promises, promises . . .*
>
> *#### emailed me a few times requesting pictures from Greece. Not sure why he wants them, I am sure he didn't have that much fun.*
>
> *Love and miss you . . . soon I will be able to say it face to face.*

We moved out of our trailers and back into tent city around the 22nd of October. It was the first place we lived and the last place we lived before leaving for home.

Journal entry October 22, 2006

> *We moved back into tents. I am focusing on coming home. I see it, I can taste it and it is keeping me going. I have learned much*

about the Army and myself. Life is filled with uncertainty right now, but I have to have faith and I thank God for giving me the strength and courage and honor.

Another soldier was kidnapped towards the end of October and I was despondent. I felt like this would never end.

Journal entry October 23, 2006

We have another soldier kidnapped. I know what will happen and it sickens me. We have had too many soldiers die and I wonder for what? So many unanswered questions, so political. As we draw closer to leaving, tensions are at their highest. It is a different tension. I think everyone wants to get the hell out of here. 30 days and counting, wish it was sooner.

Email home October 25, 2006

I mailed some foot lockers home and some boxes and I will be sending more in a few weeks. We are getting ready to leave. It could not come soon enough. I know I have so much to do when I get there, job, housing and figuring out what to do next, but at least I will be home. Counting the days to leave this tar pit. No matter what we do, it gets sucked into a mass tar pit and it does not seem to make a difference. The country has a democracy and its leadership is tied to the militias and terrorists. It is like having the Sopranos in the White House, but worse. I am getting an award . . . what a joke . . .

When I come home I will stay in a hotel until I can find a place to live. I know I could stay with you or mom or friends, but trust me, I will need to be alone and just relax. I think it will help me integrate back in the life at home. I have become the war person, and I hope I can find my way back to me.

Back in July 2006 the 172nd Stryker Brigade Combat Team's tour in Iraq was extended for up to four months by the Department of Defense, headed by the Secretary of Defense Donald Rumsfeld. Many of the units assigned to the Stryker Brigade were stationed in Baghdad. The units were heavily utilized during surge operations. In November Rumsfeld resigned. During this time I had a NBC reporter embedded with the 172nd Stryker Brigade Combat Team. This brigade was almost home when Rumsfeld extended their deployment, which caused a great deal of angst and hostility. When he resigned, the reporter wanted to interview soldiers from the 172nd about his resignation. I got a knock on my door at 2:00a.m. and was told that the reporter was about to go "live" with his broadcast and was rounding up soldiers to interview. When I arrived on location he was standing in the lights with the satellite truck fired up ready to go live. I pulled him aside and asked him not to do the story because it was not in good faith. We didn't want any negative press surrounding this event and I promised him that I would get him the next big story. To my relief he didn't do the story, shut the satellite truck down and he went back into his tent. I briefed my boss and told him I made a promise to this reporter that I hoped to keep. I was in no position to make this promise, but it was the only way to prevent the reporter from doing a negative story about Rumsfeld. I was able to get him on the next big story. A few days later a U.S. soldier was kidnapped in Baghdad and forces were looking for him. NBC got the opportunity to cover the story.

The "end of tour awards" was being processed within the section. I heard that some people were getting higher awards for the same job performance than others. The active component limited the number of higher awards to be given to our Reserve unit, with only a few people able to receive the highest award, the Meritorious Service Medal. The active duty section was allowed higher awards, including the Bronze Star Medal. When I found out what award I was to receive, I went to my commander and told him that I didn't want it. I felt like I deserved something much higher than the Army Commendation Medal, the second lowest award. As a lieutenant I worked in both captain and major positions and I prevented a major news story from unfolding when Rumsfeld resigned. If I couldn't get the award I deserved, I didn't want one. My commander told me the Commanding General of the United States Army Reserve was coming to pin on our awards so I, like everyone else, was expected to be in formation. This just added insult to injury. For me it was embarrassing and humiliating. I received the same award as the captain who was fired and the private whose only job was to sweep the floor and take out the trash. Award ceremonies are usually happy times for soldiers but not for me.

After the ceremony I walked back to my office and asked my active duty boss why I got the lowest award in the section. He gave me some bullshit explanation and I knew this situation could not end soon enough.

Our replacements arrived around the 1st of November. It was like Christmas and they were the best presents ever received. We spent two weeks training them. Most of our replacements had already been to Iraq and had worked in the same building. As we trained our replacements many of the soldiers in my unit trained their counterparts and were released from their duties. They returned to work at the Media Operations Center where life was much easier. I still kept my cell phone and worked around the clock. I was always working. My final job was to coordinate media for the transfer of authority ceremony on November 15th. Once the ceremony was completed I thought I would be released, but I continued to work full days and nights without relief.

Email home November 18, 2006

I am not sure what I will do next when I get home, but once I get there I will have to figure it out. It makes me crazy to have to think about this while I am here. The days don't go by quick enough. I so need some rest and relaxation and I need to put this behind me. I was successful here, I learned and I think I made a difference to lives of people whom I never met or met here. That is all I can hope for. Sometime the phoenix rises from the ashes and sometimes it doesn't. Our replacements are here and I just wish I could stop working and prepare myself for coming home . . . not going to happen.

Journal entry November 19, 2006

Today was my last day in hell. I turned it all over. Let it go. Maybe I can breathe. We will be heading home soon and I am anxious to get there. I remember I said to myself anyone can do a year and a year is too long. I have said farewell to too many of my friends here and it is sad, but I am sure we will stay in touch. I have survived physically, the other parts of me is yet to be determined. There are few things I got to do here that brought a smile to my face. I flew in the general's helicopter twice. Met

> *several amazing journalist and only hope I can get a job and*
> *do work like them. I witnessed amazing men and women who*
> *sacrificed it all and still had a kind word or offered a hug.*

Once I was done with work there wasn't very much to do. We loaded our supplies, cleaned and organized our equipment and tried to stay busy. Trying to leave was another nightmare. We submitted several lists of names and information to get manifested on a flight to depart Iraq. This paperwork was frequently lost. We finally got manifested on a flight but it was postponed two or three times. The more it was prolonged the more angry and upset I got. I desperately wanted to be gone from this place and all that was associated with it.

Email home November 22, 2006

> *I hope all is well and I wish I was home . . . . I really do. It*
> *is getting tougher to be here and I am too tired to continue*
> *to fight my way through it. No one knew we were coming*
> *here and now they won't let us leave.*

Finally our departure date arrived. We carried all our belongings and waited on the flight line. I watched three large groups of people board the plane and take off. It was gut-wrenching to watch people leave while I remained here. I felt like a caged lion with nothing to do but pace. After many hours of waiting we were finally called to board the plane. It was the best day in the whole year I was in Iraq.

Kuwait: Part Two

Leaving Iraq was an agonizing process and it took forever to get out of the Middle East. My anticipation was overwhelming. I remember leaving Iraq and flying to Kuwait. As we flew to Kuwait I was excited but also knew that nothing was guaranteed—we may not fly out as planned, as delays were frequent. Kuwait was simply one more obstacle standing in the way. We had our weapons with us at all times, we still walked a mile to go to the bathroom or shower and it was very cold at night. The tents and sand were the same; our routine was the same. The only difference was no one was trying to kill us with mortars or rockets. This is a big difference. We didn't have anything to do in Kuwait but wait. It provided me time to process the past year. But as soon as I began to think about Iraq I would shut it down and change my thoughts to home. I worked myself into such excitement about going home that it became paralyzing. I couldn't sleep in anticipation of home. I pictured my friends and family, and since I love traveling, all the places I would go. Since I had no real responsibilities, I took the opportunity to catch up on current events and make contact with people via email.

Email home December 3, 2006

> *Great News! We are no longer in Iraq. We are in Kuwait. It won't be long till we get to the USA. I can't wait to see you all. I want to go home and want to leave this place. I don't want to be here one more day.*

I spent time in the Morale, Welfare and Recreation (MWR) tent to check my email and watch television. I watched television with new purpose: to connect and find out what was happening in the United

States. In Iraq I was consumed with the Middle East. Now I hungered for news of home. I was sitting in the MWR tent watching television when I learned that Missouri was hit with a terrible ice storm. The airport was shut down, the National Guard called out and electricity was out across the state. *I can't be delayed,* I thought. *I can't stay here one more day. When do I get my life back?* I wanted to lie down on the floor and scream but instead I prayed the ice would melt and we would be able to fly home. As soon as I left the MWR tent I heard the good news. We would be leaving Kuwait the next day and would be in the U.S.A on December 4th.

After being in Kuwait for a few days we finally got to leave. It wasn't until we landed to refuel outside of the Middle East that I believed I was really going home. I slept the whole flight and dreamed of home—about seeing my family and friends and how happy my life would be.

Coming Home

I trained for one year to deploy to Iraq, spent one year there and thought that the mere fact that I made it home alive would be enough to survive life after war. I was mistaken.

I arrived in the USA on December 4, 2006. I was elated to finally be on American soil. I got off the plane and boarded a bus to Fort Riley, KS for out-processing. It was minus 5 degrees and snow and ice were on the ground. Because of the 8-hour time difference, I was completely jet lagged. Out-processing included medical and eye exams, briefings about benefits and turning in equipment. During my health screening it was revealed that my eye sight changed, I weighed less and had some medical issues. There was a full-length mirror in the doctor's office and for the first time I looked at myself in a mirror and was taken aback. I looked exhausted. I had dark bags under my eyes, my face had dark patches on it from the sun and my hair was streaked with gray. War had taken its toll on me.

The first night back in the U.S., I could not sleep so I bundled up and went for a run in the below freezing temperatures. It was dark and cold but I needed to run because running calmed me down. After 45 minutes, I was back inside exhausted. It was time to get up and get ready for more out-processing. I blamed jet lag for my sleeplessness, but it was also the fear of my future.

We spent four days out-processing. Towards the last day, a man talked about services and resources for depression, alcohol abuse and other support services available to those who needed it. Almost instantly, my thoughts were consumed with drinking alcohol. All I could think about during that briefing was getting home and having a drink to celebrate my homecoming. I had not had a drink in a long time and it sounded so good to me. I have never been a big drinker, and I could pass on it most of the time. For some reason, though, having a drink became a priority. I *needed* a drink. I envisioned sipping a nice glass of red wine or a vodka tonic. As he talked, I could almost taste the alcohol on my lips. All I wanted to do was get home and be away from the unit I spent 15 months with. I wanted light, non-military conversation with my family and friends whom I loved and who loved me back and a drink while I was doing it. I wanted relief, a normal life without war and all of the craziness and horrors associated with it. Those four days in Fort Riley felt like they would never end. I was done with war and wanted my normal life back. The frustration continued to build the closer I got to home. On my last day at Fort Riley, I boarded a bus around ten a.m. What should have been a 4-5 hour bus ride home took ten hours. The bus broke down twice and we were stuck in various places in Missouri on Interstate 70. It was typical of deployment and how things worked in the military. I sat on the broken bus and thought, *put a bunch of war heroes on a bus with mechanical problems and hope they make it. Here is a fine welcome home. Will this ever end? When will the military let me have my life back? When can I stop wearing this uniform and start wearing makeup and jewelry? When can I be myself again?* It was another delay and it created such disappointment. I wanted off the war ride, I wanted my life back. We stopped for fuel at a rest stop. I stretched my legs and bought some snacks. It was 2 weeks before Christmas and this was my first opportunity to buy gifts. It felt good to shop in the open. I felt free, so free that it made me cry, which is something I really didn't do anymore. It was odd that I would cry at a rest stop in the middle of Missouri.

When we finally arrived at our Reserve Center it was after 7:00pm and our families had been at the center since 1:00pm. They were tired, anxious and excited. We were met by one person from our chain of command. He gave a quick speech on the bus, handed us a thank you card and a coin and sent us on to our families and friends. His only job was to lock up the building after we left. The rest of our leadership had other things to do. I was angry. What kind of welcome home is that for soldiers?

My family and friends were standing in the drill hall. They were real and I could touch them, hug them, talk to them and see their beautiful faces. It looked like a scene out of a movie. Emotions were flying. Hugs and laughter filled the room. There was cake, flowers, signs, and people taking pictures. It was the polar opposite of what I just came from. I saw so much happiness and felt so much emotion that I forbade myself to feel in Iraq. I cried a little, but I turned it off—a trick I learned in Iraq. The celebration was short-lived. After the hugs and joys and pictures we still needed to lock things away, unpack the bus and drag ourselves and our equipment to a car. I didn't have a place to live or a job. I had no idea what was going to happen to me next. But for now I was just happy to be home. My family and friends took me to dinner at the Macaroni Grill. Being with them, laughing and drinking a glass of wine, reminded me of old times but felt different. Something had changed, though I would not understand what until later. I sensed that life as I knew it would never be the same again. I drank three or four glasses of wine without it fazing me. I didn't feel drunk, but I finally felt relaxed and the familiar "on the edge" feeling subsided. The wine went down smoothly and tasted delicious. That evening was when I began my love affair with alcohol.

I got my car back on the first day I was home. Driving to my unit the next day, I was in awe of the landscape. It was good to see the Mississippi River and the Gateway Arch again. Those landmarks meant that I was home. I was very careful about where and how I drove. I avoided trash and weaved away from pot holes. I didn't drive when I went outside the "wire" in Iraq, but my training was so embedded I just automatically did these things. I understood that I was at home, but instinctively reacted like I was still in a war zone.

My family wanted me to stay with them but I needed space and some private time. I was jet-lagged, tired and anxious. I lived in the hotel for two weeks and found comfort in my own space. I didn't have to cook or clean. There was a 24 Hour Fitness gym right next door, so I could work out anytime I wanted to. Whenever I felt anxious or restless I headed to the gym. Sometimes it would be two a.m. Other than finishing up last-minute business with my unit, I really didn't have much to do. I was not used to having this amount of free time. When you live on alert, working day and night with no break, it shocks your system to just stop and be still. Free time increased my anxiety because there was too much time to think and reflect about my experiences.

On the third day home, I spent countless hours searching for my weapon. I opened every drawer in the room and searched my suitcase. I went into a panic and broke out in a cold sweat. I couldn't find my weapon. About two hours later, I realized I was at home in a hotel and no longer in Iraq. It was very disturbing to feel this way. I instinctively walked outside my room to go to the bathroom. I would open the door and start to walk before realizing I didn't have to walk outside. Repeatedly the door shut and locked before I realized this, and I had to get a key from the front desk.

When I moved into an apartment at the end of December, I continued to spend time searching for my weapon and walking outside to go to the bathroom. I walked right out my back door and into my yard. When I saw the grass and houses I would either laugh at myself or just walk back inside and wonder what the hell was wrong with me. I felt split in two. I was having difficulty mitigating life at home.

My first two weeks at home were pretty difficult. After being home for just a week, I drove to meet a friend for coffee. It was a Sunday morning and I was driving in a neighborhood I knew quite well. I came to a stop sign and there were construction barriers and lane changes. I drove slowly, trying to get my bearings. An older man pulled up behind me and honked his horn over and over again. He then pulled up to the side of me, flipped me off, rolled down his car window and screamed at me. I was shocked and alarmed at the same time. I sat in my car and just honked my own horn for as long as he sat next to me. Anger rushed over me. I felt the adrenaline rise in my veins. I wanted to get out of my car and punch him. I knew that I had to remain in my car and maintain self-control or I would do something I would regret, despite the release hitting him would give me. It took me about 15 minutes to calm down and compose myself. When I entered the coffee shop, my friend could tell there was something wrong. I didn't tell her what happened because honestly didn't know what to say. My reaction was so over-the-top that I couldn't explain it.

Christmas was quickly approaching and I needed to buy presents so I went to World Market and filled my basket to the top. I put my items on the counter to check out and the woman in front of me gave me a dirty look for putting my items too close to hers. The clerk picked up something of mine to ring it up and she scorned, "that is not mine that is hers!" She mumbled under her breath that if I would have just waited my turn there would be no mix up. I felt anger growing. When she finished paying and walked away, I said to the clerk, loud enough for her to hear, "I just got home from Iraq and I really don't give a shit about her and would be happy to kick her ass." The woman ran out of the store. The cashier smiled at me and thanked me for my service. I was furious. If I would have met her on the parking lot, I would have given her a piece of my mind; lucky for her she was gone. I could not forget it or let it go. Strangely, this incident angered me for many months.

After I left World Market, I ventured to the mall. As I walked around, I could not help but notice that there were many overweight adults and kids everywhere. I just spent 15 months away from home with fit military men and women. In Iraq, we needed to stay in shape to stay alive. I wondered how any of these overweight people could physically defend themselves or others. I spent a year in a country that was poor and many children didn't have food to eat and were thankful for anything they may have received, but here people looked gluttonous and unaware of how valuable their bodies were. At the time, I looked at them with judgment and anger. I watched television and listened to political rhetoric only to find myself upset because our nation was divided. Where I came from, I knew that any division in our nation made the enemy stronger.

I celebrated Christmas with my family. It was surreal; while I was there physically, mentally and emotionally I was still in Iraq. I launched into a long diatribe about Iraq and Iraqi security forces, etc. One family member looked at me like I was crazy. He stopped me in mid-sentence and asked if I needed a "drink or something." I looked around and my "speech" had cleared the room. I felt very out of place and couldn't wait to go home. I preferred being alone.

To get my gas service turned on at my new apartment I needed to pay a deposit at the supermarket. There was only one person working. The person ahead of me was being difficult so it took more time than usual. I waited behind a white line on the floor. Out of the corner of my eye, I saw a woman walking quickly towards me. She looked angry and was waving money in her hand. She walked right past me in line and began tapping the money on the counter. The clerk told her to get in line; that he would wait on her as soon as possible. She huffed and got in line behind me. She stood very close to me and was talking to herself and rocking. I felt threatened because she was in my personal space, impatient and agitated. When the clerk called me to the counter, the woman walked up beside me and began tapping the money on the counter again. I turned, looked at her hatefully and told the clerk that I just returned from a war zone and if he did not ask her to move I was going to move her myself and it would not be pretty. The clerk asked her to move back in line to wait her turn. She spoke in a very agitated tone. It wasn't directed at me, but I felt like it was. I was in a cold sweat, my adrenaline was up and I was prepared to fight. She realized that I was at my limit and left. The only time I felt like myself was when I was on an adrenaline high. I realized at that moment that the only way I felt "normal" was to be in the fight or flight mode and I had to create scenarios to make myself feel "normal." Food, over-exercising and drinking were ways I learned to create a sense of relief, but when opportunities arrived that created those accelerated feelings inside of me I was happy because I felt like me again.

The honeymoon phase of coming home ended soon. The phone stopped ringing and the "welcome home" parties ended. When I first came home, I went out for coffee, dinner, lunches and happy hour. It was so exciting to see everyone and spend time with them. My phone rang all the time, people came by my apartment and it was a great. Keeping busy helped me escape from being overwhelmed and feeling out of place. When the excitement of me coming home died down and my loved one's lives returned to normal, I was left with my own thoughts and feelings.

Journal entry January 8, 2007

It has been 30 days since I arrived home. Here's what it is like so far:

Surreal—am I really here?
When do I have to go back? I think I want to go back.
Lives go on without you.
I was home for two holidays, but not interested in them. Wish I could go back to Iraq, holidays are not significant.

I made an appointment with the Veterans Administration (VA) for counseling and attend my first session. It was a good first session, but I really didn't think I would have to come back. In mid-January I had some problems with my upstairs neighbors. My sleep pattern was still off because I was in a different time zone and was used to working different shifts. My neighbors' alarm clock ran from 4:45a.m. to 7:00a.m., every day. The buzzing got louder as the alarm went through its cycles. Most nights, I would get to sleep around 4:00 or 4:30 a.m. and would be startled awake by the buzzing, unable to fall back asleep. I knocked on the ceiling and threw a shoe at the wall. I left a note requesting that they turn off their alarm after the first or second buzz. My request was ignored and for a few more weeks their alarm buzzed incessantly for over 2 hours in the early morning preventing me from sleeping. I could not believe that they would be so inconsiderate. It angered me to my core and consumed my thoughts. One morning the alarm went off only once and later I heard my neighbor's husband leave. However, around 5:30am it started again and my neighbor's wife continued hitting snooze until 7:00a.m. I was livid. I got up, put on my clothes and shoes, walked upstairs and banged on the door until my hand hurt. I screamed at her to "turn off that fucking alarm clock." Luckily, she did not come to the door. I believe that if she would have opened the door I would have punched her in her throat and pulled that alarm clock out of the wall. I was in a rage and it felt shamefully good. I headed to the gym. Though I worked out for 2 hours, I remained agitated and very, very awake.

I spent most of the day away from my apartment, running errands and shopping. That evening my neighbor's husband knocked on the door. We got into a heated fight about my behavior towards his wife. He was on the steps, hovering over me and waving his hands. I told him calmly that I would knock him off the steps if he came any closer to me. I told him I just came home from Iraq and did care about him or anything. If he wanted to fight, bring it. He stopped in his tracks. He looked at me with surprise and said that he was sorry about the alarm and it would not happen again. He shook my hand, thanked me for my service and went back to his apartment. I was in a fight mode and was confused about what just took place. I went back into my apartment, called my father in tears and asked him what was happening to me. I broke down. I just wasn't myself. I was exhausted but I couldn't sleep. I didn't belong and couldn't relate to civilians. Common irritations sent me into a rage. I wanted to fight, I wanted to scream. I was out of control. I was afraid that I was going to hurt someone. I made an appointment with the VA for more counseling. I needed more help than I realized.

Journal entry January 30, 2007

> *My incident with my neighbor screwed me up and I have hit the wall. Anxiety and anger and it came crashing down on me and I am an emotional mess. Flood of feelings and it scared me, really did. I am not sure how to handle it, my neighbor threatened me and it was all over from there. I am afraid to go home because my reality sucks. It seems to be too overwhelming for me. I feel like I don't belong. I guess I will find my place.*

While I was in Iraq I struggled with staying connected to home and when I came home I struggled with trying to fit in. In Iraq I emailed this home. I was begging for news from home and just wanted to be included.

Email home May 25, 2006

> *Ok here is another thought for you all. I know that hearing from me may be hard because of what I am going through, but ladies and gentlemen I am not dead. I want to know what is going on in your lives. I truly do. Just imagine you have been banished to an island with minimal contact and everyone decides not to contact you. You will feel lonely and out of touch. I asked some of you "will you still know me when I come home?" I have missed so much and really don't know what to expect, but I do want you all to know I think about you guys all the time and want only the best for you. It is hard here, but it has not changed who I am. I am still your friend or daughter or sister, niece etc . . . It is me, tell me what is going on with you and send pictures. I want to stay connected. I need to stay connected. Ok enough of that.*

In addition to counseling at the VA I was going to physical therapy for the leg injury I received while running from a mortar. I pulled my leg muscles around my right hip. I worked with my physical therapist, Nicole, and a recreational therapist named Jean. I was told I couldn't run for four weeks and to swim instead for cardio. Jean took me to the pool and we began swimming twice a week. I loved swimming and did it well. But for some reason I could not put my face in the water, which made swimming difficult. I never had difficulty swimming normally before I went to Iraq. I swam at the pool at the VA or the YMCA trying to overcome my fear. One day in therapy I realized why I was afraid to put my face in the water. I thought if I put my face in the water I would die. My New Year's resolution was to swim with my face in the water. It took me almost a year to put my face in the water, but I did it by the next New Year's Day.

I felt insignificant because the lives of my loved ones had gone on without me. I was at a dinner party with friends where the first 30 minutes they talked about their lives: their jobs, vacations, get together for the holidays, running 5K races, attending their children's events. I could not relate or be part of the conversation. Being at war excluded me from their lives. I was gone for almost two years. There is no machine to give time back. I wasn't there for the joyful times, weddings, births of babies, Bar Mitzvahs, baptisms, confirmations, graduations and 4th of July barbecues. I wasn't there to help them through rough patches of their lives. It was very humbling to realize that everyone lived their lives without me—and survived. I felt disconnected, alienated and unable to relate to those I knew best. My life in Iraq was joyless. It was filled with death, horror, fear, profound sadness, fatigue and sleepless nights. Who wants to hear about that? Who could relate? I couldn't have a normal conversation about my life. I didn't want be a "downer," so I plastered a pretend smile on my face, nodded politely and did my best to fit in. I wanted to stay connected and did my best to do so while I was in Iraq. I realized friends and family didn't want to burden me with their everyday problems or tell me the good things because they didn't want to make me feel worse than I did already. While their motives were good, it alienated me from their lives.

Sometimes, in moments of self-awareness, relaxed emotions and feelings would come over me like a wave. I was ready to talk about my experiences and tried to do so. On a few occasions, I spoke about my experiences to a close friend. When I finished, I asked my friend what she thought and she just shook her head. She responded that she could not relate, but would always be there for me to listen because that was something she was good at. For the first time I opened up about my life at war but the person I talked to did not know what to do. It wasn't her fault, but I realized that I couldn't talk to any of my family or friends. But I desperately needed to talk to someone. It took me a little over a month to make that appointment at the V.A. to see a therapist. Therapy was a way to let it all go. I needed a safe place to talk it out without judgment or fear. I knew there were going to be many long and lonely nights filled with sadness and anxiety.

Once, while shopping at Target, I realized I was paranoid of men and women dressed in Muslim clothing. I was shopping for items for my new apartment when I saw a woman wearing a hijab. My heart began to race. I was convinced she was going to blow up Target. I became hyper-vigilant. I grabbed for my weapon that wasn't there and wanted people to run for cover. I recognized that I was in Target, but this woman and her hijab freaked me out. I actually grew so paranoid that I left my cart and ran out of the store. Rationally I knew my response was unwarranted, but my reaction was instinctive. I needed to protect myself.

To be honest, I am still paranoid about men/women dressed in traditional Muslim clothing. Seeing them no longer causes me to flee, but I am hyper-vigilant in their presence. I know these judgmental thoughts are wrong, but my body automatically reacts. There are people in the U.S. who react this way even if they have not gone to the Middle East. This stereotype is very wrong. I have been home for more than five years and I am still working to change the way I think about this matter.

I didn't have to report to my unit for 90 days, and a lot can happen in that length of time. I started having nightmares and woke in a panic. I wandered around my apartment looking for something, feeling out of place. I was already registered at the VA and had appointments scheduled. I was adamant about having soldiers in my unit register as well. We are entitled to five years of free medical care, and I knew many of my unit members needed help like me.

I never really unpacked my boxes when I moved in. The ones I did unpack were neatly organized and labeled with loved one's names. All the boxes were symbolic and sentimental to me. I came home alive and was very happy for that. But for some reason I felt sad when I viewed the labeled boxes. I slept on box springs and a mattress on the floor. I couldn't settle down. I wanted or needed to go back to Iraq. I understood Iraq; home was something much harder to navigate. Everything seemed foreign and unfamiliar. There were different sounds now, like the sound of a city bus going by or church bells ringing. I hadn't heard these sounds in 15 months. I was being hugged and kissed by friends and family and people told me they loved me. This shocked me at first because I hadn't experienced this type of warmth and affection in Iraq. I had forgotten what it meant to be loved.

Letter to friends, December 2007

> *I found an apartment and moved in on December 29th. I had no furniture, but about 50 boxes of stuff. I gave most of my heavy furniture away before I left and lots of other things too. I still can't find things and I know someone has a nice chair or book shelf or clothing and it came from me.*

I found myself restless and unable to remain in one place. I have always loved to travel, and since I didn't have a job I decided to visit friends and get away from all the stuff that reminded me of Iraq. This was when I learned the truth behind the old saying, "no matter where you go, there you are." I enjoyed my time in California. I went to Napa Valley and felt like I had hit the jackpot in wine. I was happy to be away and drinking. It was a great vacation and escape, but I was still filled with anxiety and anger and no matter what I did to mask it, it seethed inside of me. I could feel it boil inside and alcohol released it. Wine and more wine became the answer. I couldn't escape my own feelings and when they surfaced I was scared of them, so I stuffed them back down and continue to enjoy my time visiting friends. I was so exhausted in Iraq that I thought I would sleep soundly at home; it didn't happen that way. I drank to sleep and mixed in melatonin to stay asleep. I felt like a train wreck. I knew what I was doing was wrong, but a part of me didn't care.

My command sent me to Washington D.C. to attend the Reserve Officer Association annual conference. High ranking officials, congressmen and other VIPs would be attending. It was a good place to network and meet other professionals. I was honored to be selected to attend. I met and asked the Army Reserve General of the Army Reserves what was being done to help veterans who were without medical insurance or experiencing psychological problems. His response was that there were services available, but there weren't enough to meet demand. The military was working on establishing more resources for those who needed help.

A primary topic of discussion at the conference was the stigma attached to getting mental health help. Many military men and women are concerned about being perceived as "weak," passed over for promotions or harassed for seeking counseling. Each general reinforced that there would be no negative consequences for seeking help. But I didn't believe that. When I returned from the conference I checked with my chain command and found limited resources. I was concerned about others returning from combat. Since my work history included the social service field, I had enough experience to understand I needed to get help. Most veterans are not as fortunate.

Journal entry February 13, 2007

I went to DC and had a good time, but I began drinking and I drank too much and didn't sleep. I met some great people and made some connections for potential jobs, hope they work out.

I had a few bad days. I still don't feel like I belong here and I am trying to work through it. I know friends move on and change but I need to figure out where I belong. It has been difficult to deal with. The on-set of Valentine's Day has caused some angst as well. I went to therapy today. It is snowing and cold, but it still is beautiful.

Therapy is always good, yet it stirs it all up. I just went into it and came out of it. I need to move through the feelings and not let them linger.

Complications continue . . .

Two months after I returned I drove to New Orleans to visit friends. I spent the night in Memphis before heading to New Orleans the next morning. When I arrived in Memphis it was dark and there was a great deal of construction. Confused drivers had pulled over to the side of the road. I became unexpectedly nervous, breathing heavily and panicked. I pulled over and had to get myself together before driving on. It was a very intense situation. After I calmed down I called a friend to talk it through. She asked if it was a flashback. I didn't know. I really couldn't explain why I felt the way I did, but felt vulnerable and out of control. As I sat in the traffic jam, I felt exposed, trapped and unsafe without any protection. Once I got off the highway and checked into the hotel I headed straight to the bar for a drink. I needed a drink.

While in New Orleans, I went to Mardi Gras and drank the whole time I was there. It was an expected and an accepted part of the weekend. The more I drank the less anxious I felt and the less I cared about anything. I focused on the fun and spectacle of Mardi Gras, ignoring the fact that I was developing a drinking problem.

In March my "grandmother" died. She wasn't an actual relative, but a very close family friend. She lived next door to my mother and we were significant in each other's lives. She sent me numerous cards while I was in Iraq and placed my name on the prayer list at church. She had a stroke while I was in Iraq and was in a debilitated state by the time I came home. I visited her as much as I could, and though she couldn't speak very well she recognized me every time I visited. She managed to tell me that she was glad I made it home alive and had the chance to see me. She got progressively worse and was hospitalized with congestive heart failure. Her prognosis was poor.

On March 8th I went to the hospital to say my final goodbye. I hugged her and whispered in her ear that I loved her, and that it was time for her to go "home" and be with her husband. I also whispered that I was home, was going to be okay and for her to let go. I walked out of her room and couldn't cry. I was sad that I was numb to death because of my constant exposure to it in Iraq. Death didn't have the same emotional effect it had on me before I went to war. She died on March 10th. I needed to talk to someone so I called a close friend but didn't get an answer. I left a message about my "grandmother's" death, and heard back from her nine hours later when she left a message about her troubled day. I was hurt by her indifference to my grief. By the time I received her message I was drinking.

In April I took a trip with a group of girlfriends to Cabo San Lucas, Mexico. We went sightseeing, laid in sun and I felt relaxed. We went to Cabo Wabo, Sammy Hagar's club, to dance and enjoy ourselves. I was having a wonderful time. The music had a loud, hard bass and drum mix and smoke was coming out of the walls and ceiling. I could smell the smoke, it became foggy and I couldn't see anything around me. The atmosphere reminded me of Iraq after a mortar landed. I began to freak out and did not understand what was happening to me. My heart raced, my blood felt like it was boiling and I broke out in a cold sweat. I could not remain in the club any longer so I ran out. My friends followed after me. They didn't know what to do and I felt like I had ruined their night. We went back to the hotel and I never mentioned it. I couldn't analyze myself; I just wanted it to stop. I could not explain it and knew I had to talk to my therapist about it. During therapy, I learned that what I had experienced at the club was a panic attack. Panic attacks happen when veterans are exposed to something that reminds us of our traumatic environment. In my case, the smoke, loud bass and inability to see triggered my attack.

Shortly after returning from my vacation, I started a new job at the Reserve Center in St. Louis. I was also taking command of the unit that I had just deployed with. After being away from the unit and the Army for a few months, I must have forgotten about the negativity and disorganization. I was a desperate for a job. I think I also took this position because I was used to the chaos and drama in Iraq and taking another military job felt normal. The situation was not ideal. I didn't realize it at first, but by the end of May I knew taking this position was a mistake. This became evident when I was scheduled to go out of town for training. When I arrived at the airport I didn't have a ticket issued for travel because no one faxed my orders to the travel agency and I was unable to fly out. I called my boss to explain my dilemma and she hung up on me. I knew at that moment that I had made one of the biggest mistakes of my life. I needed to get away from this environment. It wasn't good for my physical and psychological health.

In May I went to a restaurant with a group of people to celebrate a friend's birthday. It was a great place with good food and everyone was having a wonderful time. Some of the guests were in the political business and discovered I had recently returned from Iraq. A group began discussing the war in Iraq and it was evident there were many mixed feelings. I was asked a number of questions and I answered them with honesty and frankness. When I didn't answer some of the questions with the "right" answers, I was hit with a barrage of combative comments as though I didn't know what I was talking about. I was stunned. No one at the table had been to Iraq, yet my opinions and experiences were dismissed without a second thought. The discussion was not appropriate for the venue and it became uncomfortable. I dropped the subject and avoided eye contact with anyone. I wanted to leave, but couldn't muster up the energy to do so, so I poured another glass of wine.

June was an interesting month. An email battle began and continued for months and led to the end of a long friendship. Our problems began in March when she was indifferent to my "grandmother's" death and it was never resolved. In an email to her I expressed my frustration and wrote about looking for a new job and applying for positions. Instead of responding in a helpful and supportive way, she was dismissive and belittling. We continued to banter back and forth via email instead of talking face to face. One day the emails stopped and the friendship ended. I valued our friendship. In Iraq I walked across "mortar alley" to the PX to buy her a birthday card. I even took the time to order flowers and have them delivered to her while I was in there because she was really important to me. It was really difficult reestablishing my life after war. Before war, I probably wouldn't have ended such a good friendship over something small. But what I needed from friends was basic support, patience and kindness. I believe that this friend in particular was used to being on the receiving end of support and had difficulty reciprocating because she was always in crisis and was used to having the spotlight on her. When I returned, our roles were reversed and neither of us had the patience to deal with it. I was too broken and she was too self-absorbed. When I returned from Iraq, I found out who my true friends were.

I was released from physical/recreational therapy in June. I was able to run again without restrictions. I tried to run at least 3 times a week and I struggled with it. My leg didn't hurt, but I felt out of shape and out of step. I was out of sync physically with myself. Though I spent countless hours at the gym, I couldn't figure out what my problem was with running. In late June I planned to run a 5K race at the VA called "Sweat with the Vets." I felt anxious about the race. I was pretty emotional as I ran, so I stopped running. I ended up walking with my mom and we just talked about my feelings. I was still in counseling and I talked to my therapist about my situation. I came to the conclusion that I had pent up my emotions for a very long time and that they were coming out of me, anytime, anywhere and I didn't have control over them. I realized that I needed to figure out how to control them and allow them to happen appropriately.

After being home about 7 months, I still felt out of sorts. I was still in therapy, but continued to drink excessively, exercise too much and over eat. I continued to work at the Reserve Center and it was miserable. It was the same negative work environment I had in Iraq except no one was getting killed or mortared. I knew I couldn't remain at the job very long and was looking for other opportunities. A friend of mine, a professor at a local university, told me about a Graduate Teaching Assistant program in the Communications department. I looked it up on-line and made some calls. I submitted my application, completed an interview and was accepted. I would be starting classes soon and finally had a reason to resign from the Reserve Center. I saw some light at the end of the tunnel. I looked forward to a fresh start.

Independence Day used to be my favorite holiday. I loved the picnics, parties, fairs and fireworks. But my first 4th of July home was traumatic.

I attended a party with some family members at a casino that is located in the downtown area near the Gateway Arch. The casino floated on the Mississippi River providing us with front row seats to the fireworks show. I was excited about being with my family and having such a wonderful view. The show began shortly after the sunset. As the fireworks exploded, I freaked out. I broke into a cold sweat and my heart raced. My father was very concerned. When he asked me what was wrong, I couldn't respond. I was frozen in a panic and was confused about why my body was reacting like this. I went inside the boat and moved down a level thinking that I would feel better but that only made it worse. The reverberation from the fireworks shook the boat even harder. I didn't know what to do. I eventually went back to the deck and held my father's hand. He comforted me and allowed me to feel the way I did. I left after the fireworks ended because I was exhausted mentally and physically. The 4th of July, the holiday, I loved the most, was ruined.

In Iraq, over time, I became desensitized to the sensations of war but the fireworks brought back all of my fears. Even now when I attend events that have fireworks I have to make a conscious effort to remind myself where I am and that I am safe. Last year was the first year since I returned that I enjoyed a fireworks show and was happy to celebrate Independence Day like I did in the past.

At some point I hit rock bottom. I was down and depressed. I no longer fit in my life and was confused. I thought, *who am I? What am I doing?* While there were many good things happening to me—I was accepted into a Master's degree program on a full scholarship and I had family and friends—I still felt like I didn't belong. I had been going to therapy regularly, but nothing seemed to change. Since I had resigned from my job at the Reserve Center I had too much time to think. I reviewed my life over and over in my head and was plagued with negative thoughts. I wanted to run away from my life and be someone else. I could no longer cope with my feelings. For the first time in my life I considered suicide. I thought about it and dismissed it. I couldn't do it. But the feelings of not belonging and not feeling like me continued. I felt like a freak. No one in my close circle of friends went to war so no one understood what I was going through. I was losing friends and isolating myself more and more. I felt like I needed to be somewhere I belonged and that place wasn't home. Maybe I needed to return to Iraq or deploy to Afghanistan. I applied for jobs in Iraq and for positions far away from St. Louis. I wanted to run away. To be somewhere I understood. I just wanted to be someone else and do something else. I tried my best to go back to Iraq where I felt I belonged. Luckily I didn't get a position in Iraq because deploying again would prolong my healing process. I met the Devil and had to decide which direction I would take. I could continue on the path I was on and end up becoming a fat, depressed alcoholic or I could focus on the changes I needed to make. I chose to heal.

I started school in mid-August and my schedule was flexible. I had plenty of time to see my counselor for therapy and my physical and recreational therapists for my physical problems. I saw my counselor twice a week and decided to be completely honest with her. I disclosed my drinking problem and my on-going feelings of depression. For the next 4 months I worked on discovering my triggers and finding healthy ways to cope. At first it wasn't easy and I would revert back to my old methods of coping. For example, when I felt anxious or overwhelmed, I turned to alcohol for relief. I don't think it was a physical addiction, but I associated having a drink with relaxation and that is what alcohol provided. Through counseling, journaling and positive thinking I was able to pull myself out of my "black hole" and begin creating the good life I deserved. Instead of turning to alcohol as my stress reducer I found alternatives. I re-learned how to meditate, turned to my journal to write about my feelings and drank hot chocolate at Starbucks. During this time I felt a renewal of my spirit and was beginning to feel like my old self.

I felt a pressing need to work in my community to give back. Helping others was missing from my life. I also wanted to meet other professionals who shared similar interests and who could be positive role models for me. I found opportunities to attend events and met women leaders in my community. At one particular event I was inspired by the guest speaker. I purposely stayed after the event to meet her and discuss my goals. She told me about the Women in Leadership program in my area and encouraged me to apply. I applied for the program and was accepted. I started the program in January 2008.

I sent out my first holiday letter to all my friends and family. I wrapped up my year and told some of my "secrets" about deployment. Overall, I felt like things were changing for the better.

Holiday Letter to friends and family December 2007

It is that time of year when we send out cards and gather friends and family to celebrate the holiday season. I have never sent one of these "letters" out before but I felt it was necessary for me to do this year. This might be a long one, so grab a hot chocolate and read on.

This year was a very special year for many reasons. As you all know I returned from Iraq on December 8, 2006. Time has flown since I have returned. Time didn't move quickly when I was in Baghdad. It seemed to have stood still. It was groundhog's day. I ate the same things daily, slept in the same 5x2' trailer, took a shower in the same place, and worked in the same building with the same people 24 hours a day, 7 days a week. Sounds similar to home, not really, I was in Iraq and in the middle of a war. Til this day I am still amazed that I went to war. Can any of you believe it? Some days I remember it well and others I choose to forget. But I know deep down inside of me I was there. It changed me. Some good, some not, but I know as time goes . . . it will be for the better. I do see life differently. I know the value of it and how no matter hard life gets, we will get through it. Hope is always there and I have hope.

Since December 2006 lots of things happened. So let me share my life with you since all of you are the reasons I came home and have survived the madness of war.

December 8, 2006 we arrived by bus. I had no place to live and really had no idea what I would do with my life. It actually was not a reality to me. I felt for many months that somehow I would go back, that this was a temporary stop and back to Iraq I would go. I lived at the Drury Inn for about two weeks and then my friend Susan T. opened her house to me and I crashed there until I found an apartment. I moved into my apartment on December 29th. I had no furniture, but over 50 boxes of stuff. I gave most of my heavy furniture away before I left. I gave lots of other stuff away too and I still can't find things. I know some of you have a nice chair or book shelf or clothing somewhere that came from me. (:

Adjusting to life back here was difficult. I could not sleep for weeks, not only was I still living in the Iraq time zone, I heard buses and birds and church bells, which I hadn't heard for over a year. I could sleep with gun fire and helicopters flying over my head, but not with birds chirping in my windows and church bells ringing. It took me 7 months to get some sleep, but I still have nightmares, so sleep gets to be a scary idea, but believe me I have come a long way. I love to sleep and I have a year's worth of sleep to catch up on . . .

. . . I worked with the Reserve unit on and off throughout the year and then took a full time job in late April and I ended up quitting in August. Too much drama and I really needed to separate myself from the Army and doing the full time thing. I am still in the Reserves (1 weekend a month, 2 weeks in the summer) but I wanted my life back. I wanted a life without the constant reminder of war, a life where there is happiness. I missed you all when I was away. I had such a hole in my heart, which is now filled because I am back with you.

I started graduate school and I am working as a teacher's assistant. It has been a great way to adjust back to life and work on my master's in communications. It has been fun so far. I am not used to the homework and competition. I should graduate May 2009 and who knows where my life will take me. I start an internship January 2008 and it is working at various agencies that are involved in the community at various levels. It is a great opportunity and hopefully will land me a job where I can strive to make change for the good of our community.

So in a nutshell I am so grateful to be home and with every one of you. I have missed you all so much. I survived these last two years because of you. I came home to new babies and new marriages, and for me a new life. I get to make my life whatever

I want it to be and I know this for sure I want all of you in it. I am me because of you.

Thanks for all your love and support and know it is reciprocated 1000 times.

Love and peace to you all.

By the end of 2007 I was starting to relax and find my place. I no longer turned to alcohol to cope with my problems. I still had my ups and down but life became easier because I was sleeping more and developed a routine. I still had issues but was feeling much better. In January 2008 I decided to reduce my counseling to once a month. My time was filled with school, my part-time teaching assistant position and the Women in Leadership program. Since I had made progress psychologically, was feeling better and was busy, I thought I could take a break from counseling. My deep depression had lifted, but I still felt a level of sadness that wasn't going away. I reverted back to some of my old coping methods and justified them because I was busy doing positive things with my life.

That's when I made that New Year's resolution to swim and put my face under the water. I enjoyed the Women in Leadership seminars. I was learning about good leadership skills. It was nice to have some of my own beliefs about leadership validated. I didn't go to counseling in February, and by March I was feeling overwhelmed and out of control again.

Journal entry March 30, 2008

I've been doing lots of thinking and I am back in therapy. Seems I am depressed, go figure. I've been home 1 year and 3 months and it seems like I am not making any progress, yet I know I have done lots of work. I have regained my compassion for others and deep down I am a good person. I, right now, am lonely. I feel deprived, almost depleted of love, not that I don't have it in me, I just need to feel it. I wonder why I have these feelings and why they are so strong for me right now? I had a good weekend, filled with lots of activities and drinking. I think I need to stop it. Really. I have been running and still want to lose weight. I eat when I am bored, eat when I am at home, eat

when I am sad. I just need to fill my time. I do stuff all the time,
but sometimes I don't want to do any of them. I think I am the
poster child for walking depression.

I appeared to be doing okay but I still suffered in silence. I began talking about my experiences to my family and friends. I usually started the conversation by telling them that they didn't need to do anything but listen to me. That seemed to make things easier for all of us. I talked to my friend, Beth, for a very long time. I told her anything and everything that came to my mind about Iraq and how I was feeling. I finally admitted to her that I thought about suicide because I felt like I didn't belong here or anywhere anymore. As soon as I said it, I felt free. I realized that I had kept that feeling inside of me. I was ashamed that I ever thought about suicide. I never acted on or planned my suicide but by verbalizing it, something changed within me. It was a major breakthrough.

When I returned from Iraq it took a long time for me to feel safe at home. Carrying my weapon in Iraq gave me a sense of security. At home, without my weapon, I felt unsafe and insecure. While I was in school I started to dog sit. When a professor was out of town his dog, Louie, stayed overnight in my apartment. I slept so well that night, it felt miraculous. I finally felt safe. That's when I knew I wanted a dog, but wasn't sure if it would be a good fit for me. I was in the military, in school and my life was pretty hectic. But the thought stayed with me, and I let people know that was interested in having a dog.

Journal entry April 7, 2008

I ran a half marathon yesterday. It was a good run, hilly, but
I did it. I feel recovered enough to run some more, but I will
rest today and run tomorrow. I went out on a date. Met him
for coffee. It was nice. I am not going to get caught up in this; I
just need to take life one day at a time. I was slightly weepy over
the weekend, not sure what is happening. I slept pretty well.
Miracle. I was up at 7am and ready to go. I haven't felt this
good in a few weeks. I emailed someone about helping with my
book. Let's hope it works out. I am watching my food intake. I
know it is related to stress. Successful has taken on a different
meaning to me and I am struggling with this. I don't see myself

as successful right now, but I know I have done some amazing things. When people ask me what I do and I reply "student" it feels weird. I sort of feel I lost time in Iraq and should be further along. I just need to figure out what I will do with my life. I know I want to be active in my community and help people, but do it at a larger level. Help vets, help the military. I don't know.

At the end June of 2008 I headed to the Virgin Islands with some friends and had a lovely time. It was an amazing trip and I found some peace and solace in the ocean. I got to sail, snorkel and enjoyed my friends and the beauty of the islands. I felt like my old self again. During my vacation, I got a call from my professor who told me he found a black Labrador retriever in his backyard. He said that he didn't have any tags but he was a good, gentle dog. He wanted to know if I could foster him for a little while until we could find him a home. I agreed to do it. I got home from vacation on July 1st and went to meet the dog on July 2nd. Upon meeting this dog I knew I would keep him for myself. I named him Mulligan which means "second chance." I scheduled his surgery and picked him up the next week. I wasn't sure what I had gotten myself into, but it felt right.

I picked him up on a Wednesday, and he was neutered and anxious. I knew what it felt like to be anxious so I empathized with him. I had not had a dog since I was a kid. I didn't read the instructions on his medical discharge paperwork telling me to limit his food and water intake. When he entered my apartment he went right for the water bowl and full food dish. He ate and drank until he couldn't eat or drink anymore. Ten minutes later he threw up all over my apartment. I started to cry. I didn't think I could take care of a dog. I thought I had made a mistake, but I kept him. He began to gnaw his stitches and we ended up back at the Humane Society for medical care. He returned wearing a cone around his head. With the cone, he scraped paint off the wall. Since he couldn't see well with the cone on he accidentally ran into me and the cone cut the back of my legs. Fortunately, after two weeks, we finally settled in. We established a routine. I knew I made the right decision by adopting him—he became my best friend. Mulligan saved my life as much as I saved his. It took me a few months to get used to being responsible for another living being but I finally got it down. He kept me from hanging out late at night and drinking. He made sure I got up early to walk him. Since he was a lab he had lots of energy and I had to run with him every day. I didn't have a fenced in yard, so I had to take him to the dog park and keep him exercised. A few times, at the beginning, I regretted getting him when I realized the commitment he required. But I have not regretted getting him since. I have had him for three years now and he has brought me so much happiness. He gives my life purpose and I love him. My professor, Joe, who found Mulligan helped save my life by making the request for me to foster Mulligan. It is funny how things work out.

In August 2008 I transferred into the Army National Guard. I needed exposure to different people and a different position in the military. As soon as I entered the National Guard I was sent to Louisiana for State Emergency Duty. I was off to a fresh start, working in a new position and happy to be there.

I was able to merge my "war life" with my current life and felt like I survived war and all its consequences. I found a renewed sense of purpose in my life. My life came together. I felt connected to myself, my friends and family and my community. I was still in school, working at my teacher's assistantship and was offered a part-time contracting job at a non-profit agency. I moved away from my bad coping habits and found new relief with meditation, massage and chiropractic services. I found happiness again.

Journal entry January 22, 2009

> *I have not written since July 2008. Life has been absolutely crazy and good at the same time. Yin and Yang, always. Trying to keep life balanced. I got called to State Emergency Duty in Baton Rouge, LA last September and it was a long 15 days. Reminded me of Iraq in some ways. But we made a difference and helped a community. I made contact with the media in that area and was able to get their Louisianan Public television station out to do a video on the 203rd. Louisiana Live. It is always good to see soldiers doing what they do best. I rescued Mulligan in July and I never thought I could love something so much. It was an adjustment for me, but I am glad he is in my life. The holidays were the best ever. I am starting to like them again.*

In 2009, I fell in love and graduated with my Master's degree in Communications. My life finally felt normal. It was filled with the usual ups and downs, but I could manage them without much difficulty. I felt a true sense of belonging. I love to travel and so I decide to plan a trip for my birthday and invited a group of friends to Las Vegas. In January 2010 we flew to Vegas and had the time of our lives. We shopped, ate delicious food and enjoyed the sites. A group of us went to a Cirque Du Soleil show. It was supposed to be enjoyable, but a certain scene caused me to have a flashback. A man in the show set himself on fire and walked around the stage. It reminded me of when I witnessed a man burn alive after his vehicle was struck by IED. I experienced the same feelings and emotions I had when I was in Iraq, but I knew that I wasn't there. The man on stage was a performer and that it wasn't real. My friend noticed I was distressed and didn't know what to do. I was upset, but was able to calm myself down quickly using deep breathing techniques and positive self-talk. All my counseling and hard work allowed me to move through this situation much more quickly and it didn't stay with me long. Situations like this still come and go and I am sure they will for the rest of my life, but I am ready for them and can handle them with positive outcomes.

War broke me, I broke it and at some point on my journey I finally found my place and purpose. War will always be part of me, but I know now I am not war.

EPILOGUE

War would never be synonymous with butterflies, sunshine or rainbows. I understood that from the beginning. When I arrived in Iraq, I learned about war and all its intricate workings. War was constant crisis. I thought if I could just come home alive I would return back to the life I had before I went to war. I was mistaken. Surviving war is more than just coming home. It took me about a year and a half to find my way back to myself. After the initial excitement of returning home, I came face to face with some very powerful feelings and emotions. I had enough self-awareness to seek professional help right away, but at the same time I was coping with my anxiety and depression by self-medicating with alcohol, over exercising and eating too much. I am not proud of how I handled my feelings, but my unhealthy coping techniques allowed me to temporarily relieve my stress and negative emotions. I knew that I wanted my old life back—the life before Iraq, the life without depression, anxiety and feelings of homicide and suicide. I just wanted relief and to feel "normal" again. I struggled between maintaining good positive coping skills and going back to the negative ones. It was much easier, in the beginning, to pour a glass of wine, workout to excess or over eat to avoid my feelings than it was to deal with them. I had to make a decision to move forward and find myself again or to stay where I was, stuck and alone. I chose to move forward and heal myself physically, emotionally, psychologically and spiritually.

My journey was not easy. I still find myself going back to the coping skills that I used in the past. However, I am much more self-aware now and chose healthier ways to cope. I will call a friend to talk about what I'm feeling, walk my dog or just take a minute to think before I act. I still struggle with food. I eat when I am happy, sad, angry or bored, but I have put checks and balances in my life. I use a food log, I have a personal trainer who I answer to and I am still in the military which requires me to maintain a certain weight and physical fitness level. I drink alcohol socially on occasion; not to quell anxiety or insomnia like I did in the past.

I went to Veterans Assistance for help. I received counseling and physical and recreational therapy. I found that I needed to continue to serve others and work in my community. I began taking care of myself and valuing my mind, body and spirit. I allowed myself to cry again and set realistic physical activity goals that prevented injury. Finding my way back to myself did not happen overnight. I can't rush the process. I did the work in steps and over time I felt better. There is no magic formula. I explored churches, physical activities, talked to my friends and family and allowed my feelings to flow through me. I stopped being hard on myself and began realizing how valuable my life is.

Writing this book has been an emotional process. I have been writing this book for almost five years and have re-lived everything that I have written in this book. I learned how far I have come and discovered that I still have work to do. I have battled the worst and seemed to come out ahead. I am a survivor of war and a survivor of life after war. I am resilient.

My hope is that others can find their way to start the healing process or continue on their path of healing. Re-entering life after war was difficult, but there is life after war and it can be a good one filled with joy, peace and happiness.

Michelle Matthews is currently a Captain in the Missouri National Guard and works at the Crime Victim Advocacy Center, a non-profit agency, as the Director of Training and Education. She has a Master's degree in Communications from the University of Missouri-St. Louis and a Bachelor's degree in Psychology from St. Louis University. She has served the U.S Army for 16 years including active duty, the U.S. Army Reserves and the National Guard. She wanted to write and publish this book for two reasons. First, for cathartic reasons. She believes that writing about her journey before, during and after war will allow her to release her emotions and feelings about her experiences. She is dedicated to self-growth and found writing this book healing. Second, she believes that giving a "voice" to surviving war will allow others to find their "voices" and begin to heal from war. Having her own thoughts and feelings validated was the beginning of her healing process. War is very difficult and coming home is hard to navigate. It is life changing and very challenging, but through support, patience, love and lots of work Michelle believes that anyone can live a normal life after war. She continues to survive life after war and wants to help others do the same. The book cover was designed by her friend Stephanie Arndt. Michelle told Stephanie her vision for the book cover and through her expert graphic design skills Stephanie brought her vision to life. Stephanie has designed compelling designs for authors, not-for-profits and businesses.